Bruce Mitchell

A Collection of Artworks

Compiled by Mary Mitchell

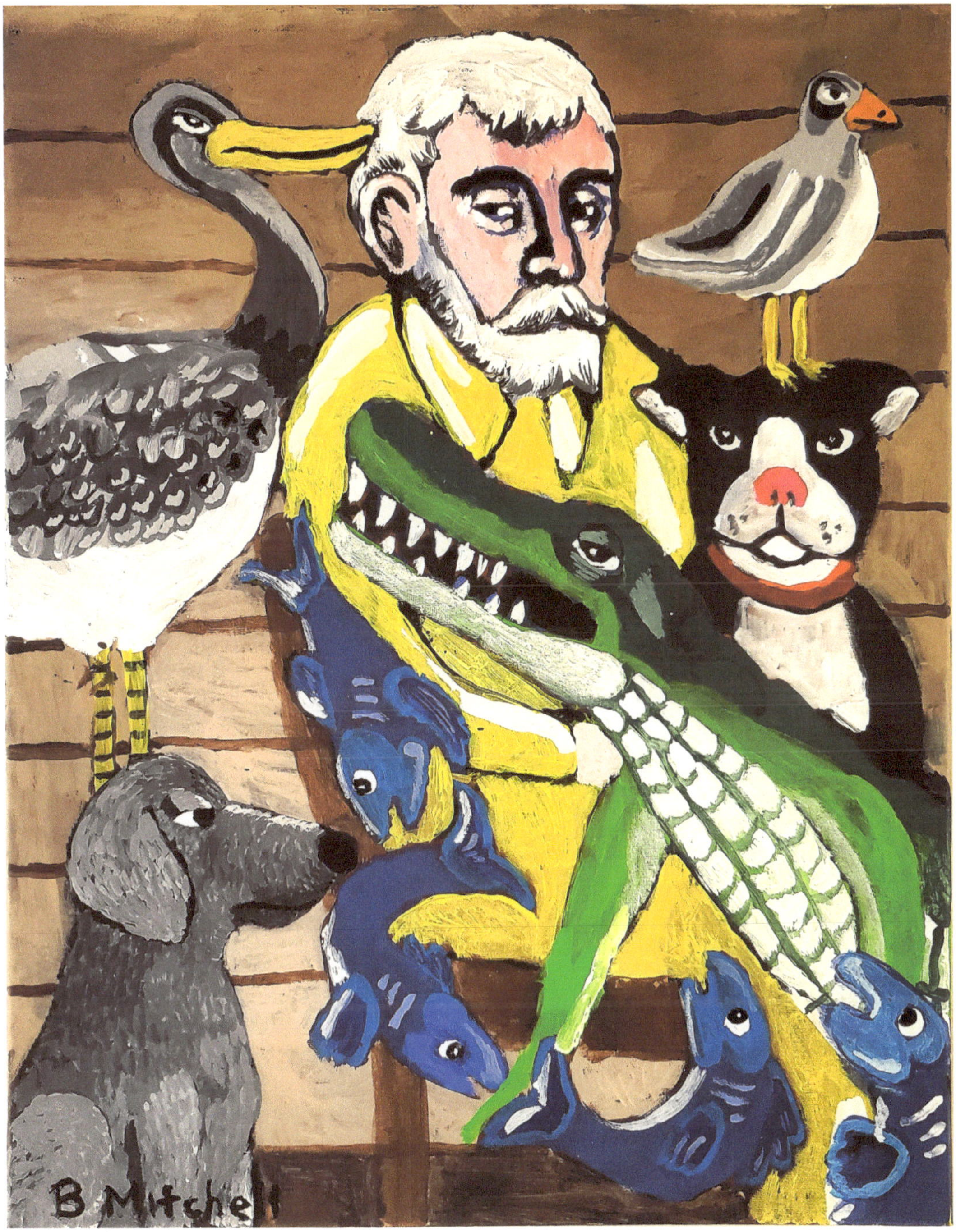

Bruce Mitchell

A Collection of Artworks

brucemitchellartwork@gmail.com

A celebration of the paintings of Bruce Mitchell 1974 - 2020

Thank you to all the people who provided us with photographs of Bruce's paintings and a special thanks to Rachel De Leon for the stories about Bruce and the work you put into the Art Program at the Mustard Seed Church.

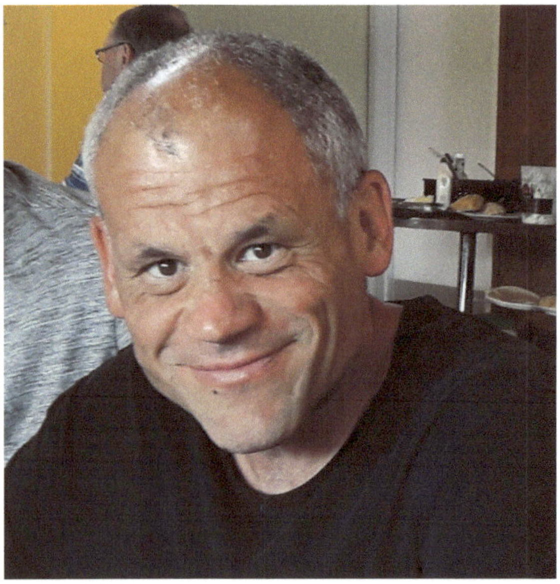

This book contains a collection of artworks by Bruce Stephen Mitchell. The primary goal of this book is to share Bruce's work with friends, family and anyone who may enjoy his creations.

Bruce was born January 24, 1974 in Edmonton, Alberta. We three Mitchell children (Bruce, Peter and I) were raised and attended school in St. Albert, a suburb of Edmonton.

Our mother is very artistic and was often engaged in creative endeavours such as watercolour painting and stained glass while we were growing up. She spent a lot of time teaching us to draw, paint, and otherwise encouraging us to create. Thanks to this enriching environment we learned to draw at a very early age.

We were more "spirited" than most children. However, one quiet activity we would partake in, especially on rainy days at the lake, was drawing. My mother would put a large pad of flip chart paper on the table and Bruce, Pete, and I would draw together on the same page. One of our favorite drawing activities was a contest to see who could draw the funniest characters. They were primarily based on people we knew such as our neighbor "Chubba bubba" who would not let children cut across his lawn. Bruce would always have the best pictures. I always assumed that when I grew up, I would be able to draw the same funny characters, or better yet superior characters. This was not the case; Bruce had a unique ability.

One of our favourite cartooning victims was our father and he was often depicted failing at simple activities. Humour was important in our family and my father encouraged a battle of the wits. Bruce could draw a delightfully insulting depiction of either of our parents with ease. For many years Bruce wanted to be a comedian and would often practice his late night host routine. This sense of humour is reflected in many of his paintings, and his sketchbooks are filled with satirical characters. Bruce would often be the quiet observer in large, boisterous family gatherings. This personality trait likely contributed to his ability to capture the essence of an individual.

With age Bruce's characters progressed. He expressed many of his beliefs in watercolour, eventually transitioning to acrylics, where he poked fun at society's problems, art and politics. He studied the masters in detail and practised his painting skills on a continuous basis. He participated in the Mustard Seed Art Program and as his skills progressed so did his confidence.

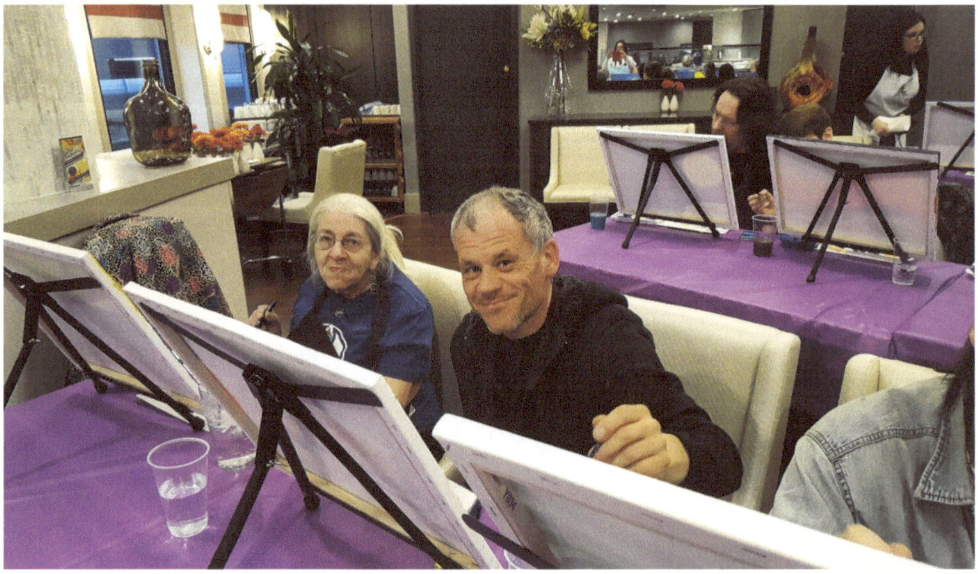

Bruce and with fellow painters at the Mustard Seed.

As we grew older, Bruce and I had less in common, but art was something we could continue to share. I would often ask both him and my mom for guidance on my own paintings and then take his advice. Although he shared the pieces he was working on, he did not share very much about other aspects of his life or his successes. Upon his death we discovered that former Alberta Premier Rachel Notley had used one of his paintings for her annual Christmas card to her riding. We also learned that he volunteered at the Mustard Seed Church Art program helping other aspiring artists in the community.

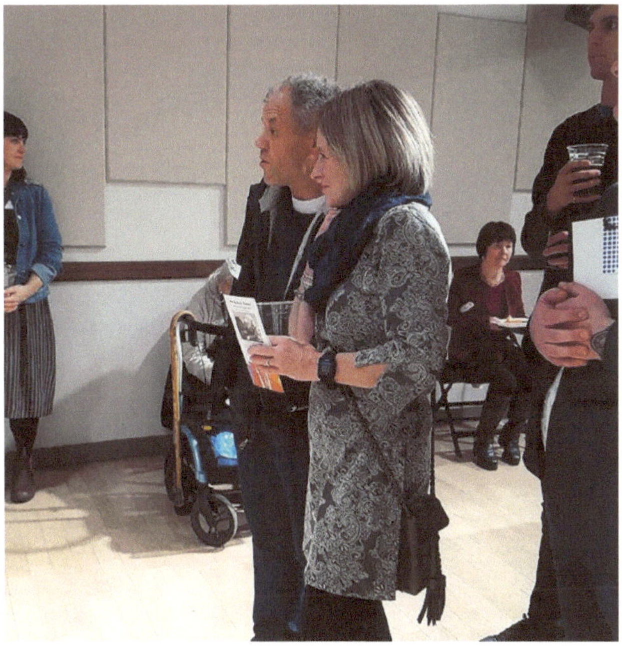

Bruce and former Alberta Premier Rachel Notley at the "Art for the Unknown" show.

Bruce did not attend art school but spent extensive time in the library downtown studying. He was well read and interested in many topics with a range of interests from art, philosophy, sociology and the American political system. His sketchbooks are full of notes on these topics and he loved to debate them with friends and family. Many of the people in his downtown community commented on Bruce's constant questioning about life. Bruce's life downtown is reflected in most of the pieces in this book. One can only imagine some of the colourful characters that must have inspired some of the scenes depicted.

Our family is grateful that he was able to produce his paintings as they have left us with a joyful memory of him. Every time I look at the Noah's Ark painting on my wall and the pissed off look of the dogs it cracks me up. I imagine him having a good laugh while working on it. I feel as though he is questioning the plausibility of having all those animals together and how Noah would have felt.

While Bruce did not always take care of himself, people remember him being very kind to others. Bruce was a gentle, artistic soul who loved dogs, art, politics, his family and friends. He will be remembered and missed by all that knew him. We hope you will enjoy the works in this book as much as we do.

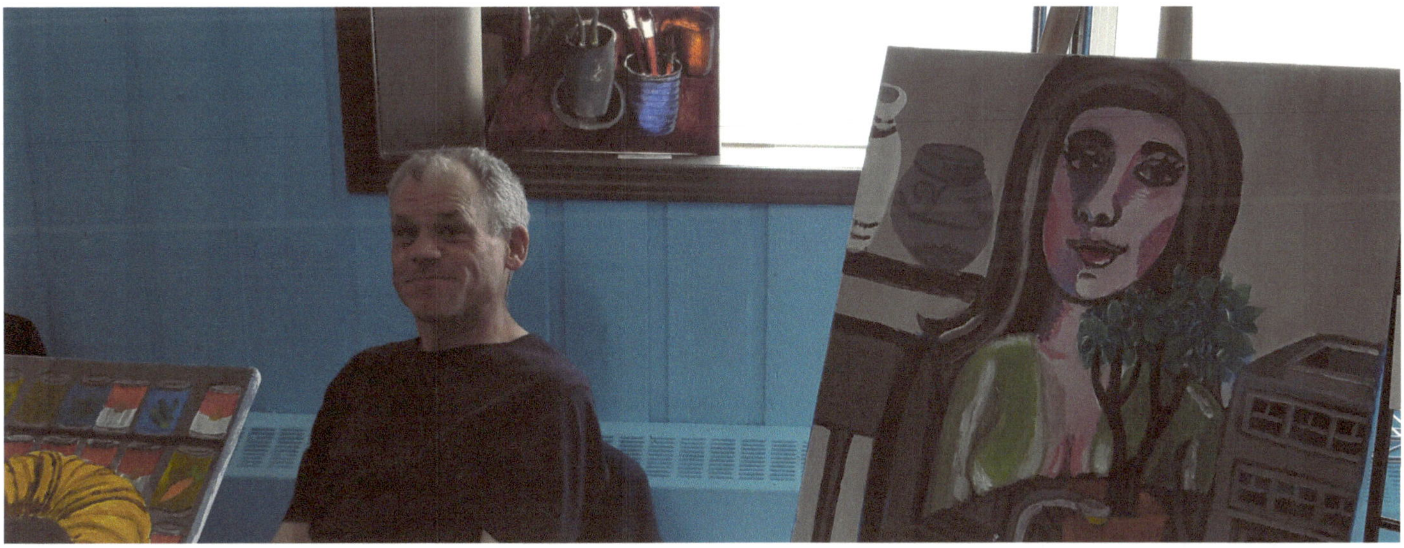

Bruce with some of his work

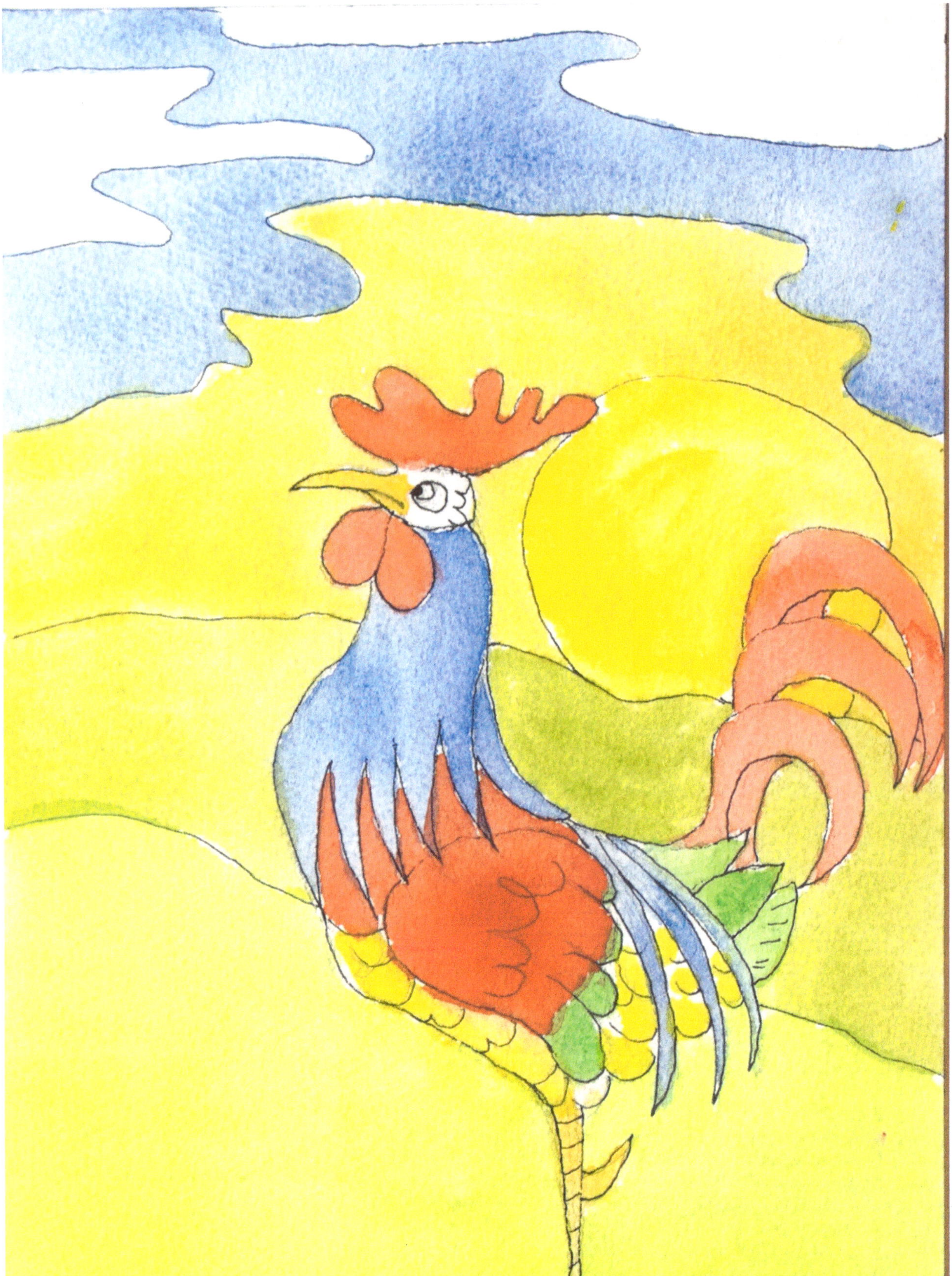

Untitled, ca. 2004. Watercolour

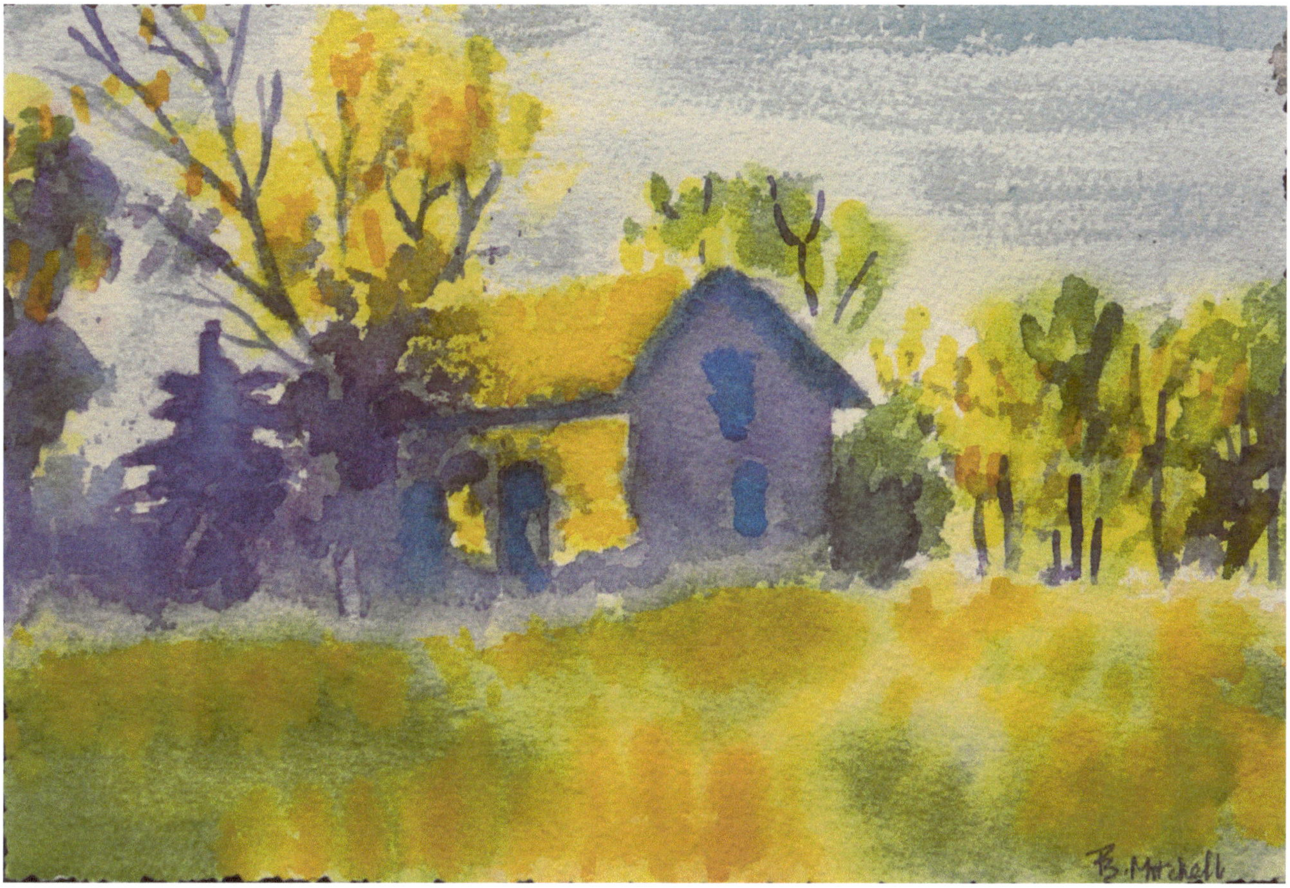

Untitled, ca. 2004. Watercolour

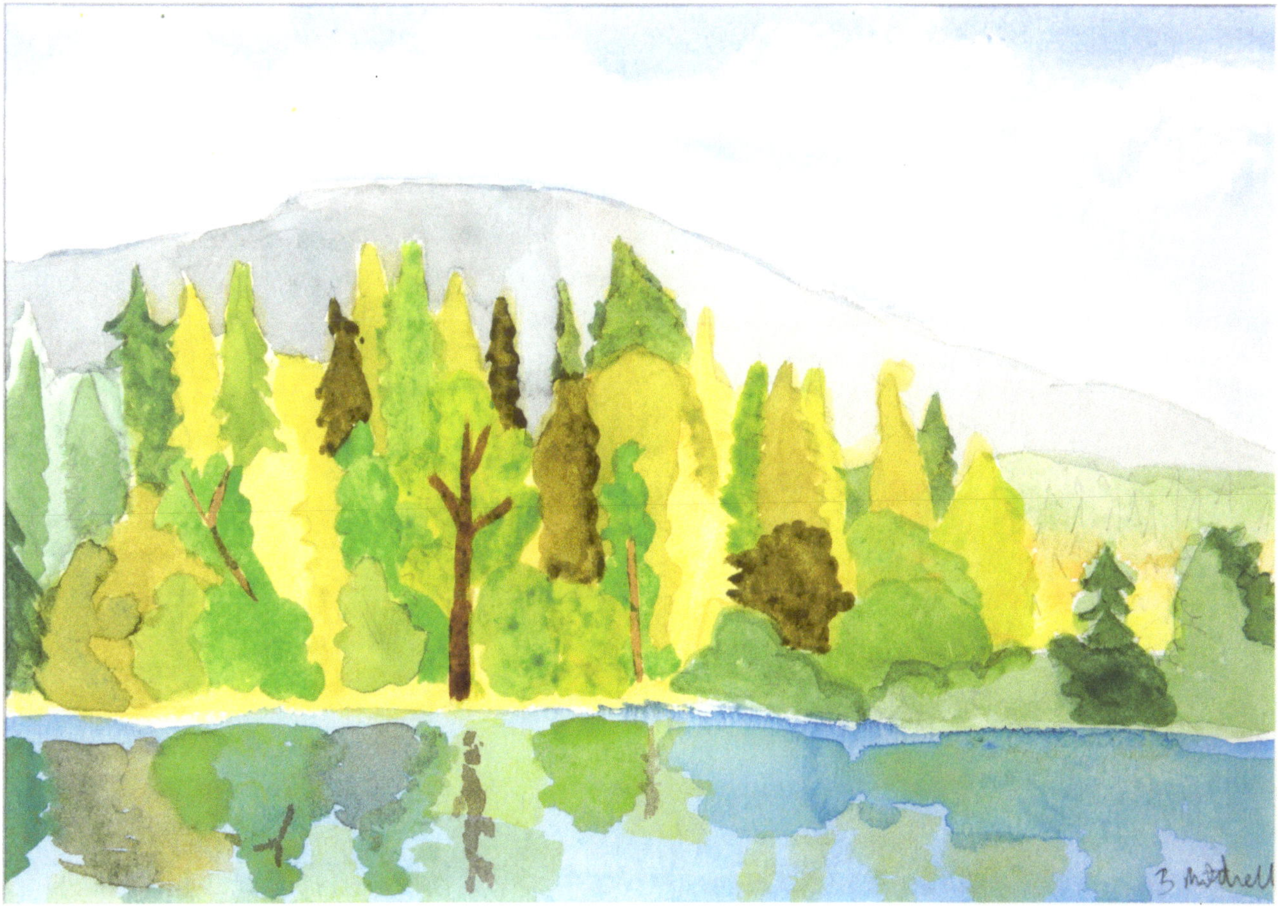

Untitled, 2004. Watercolour

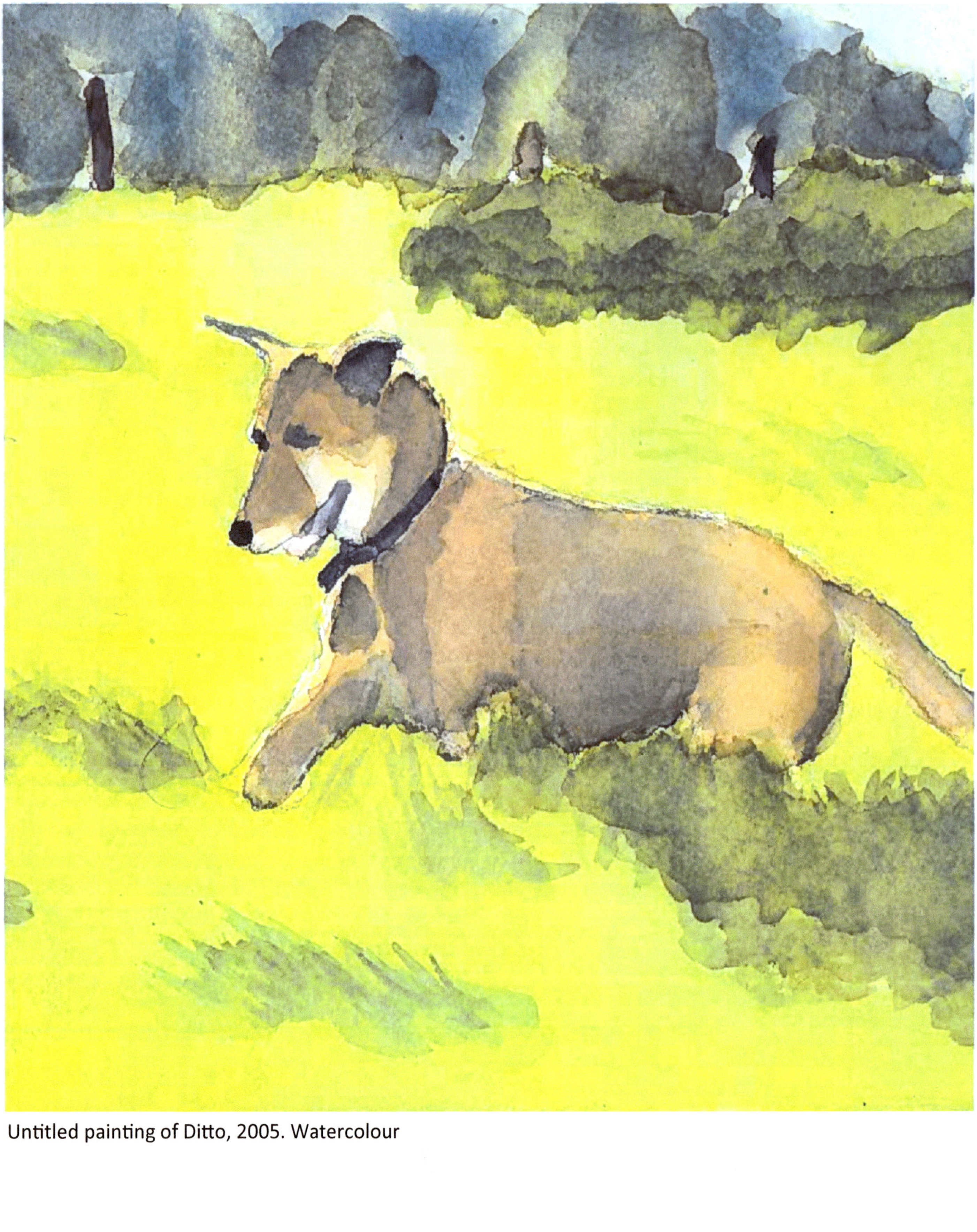

Untitled painting of Ditto, 2005. Watercolour

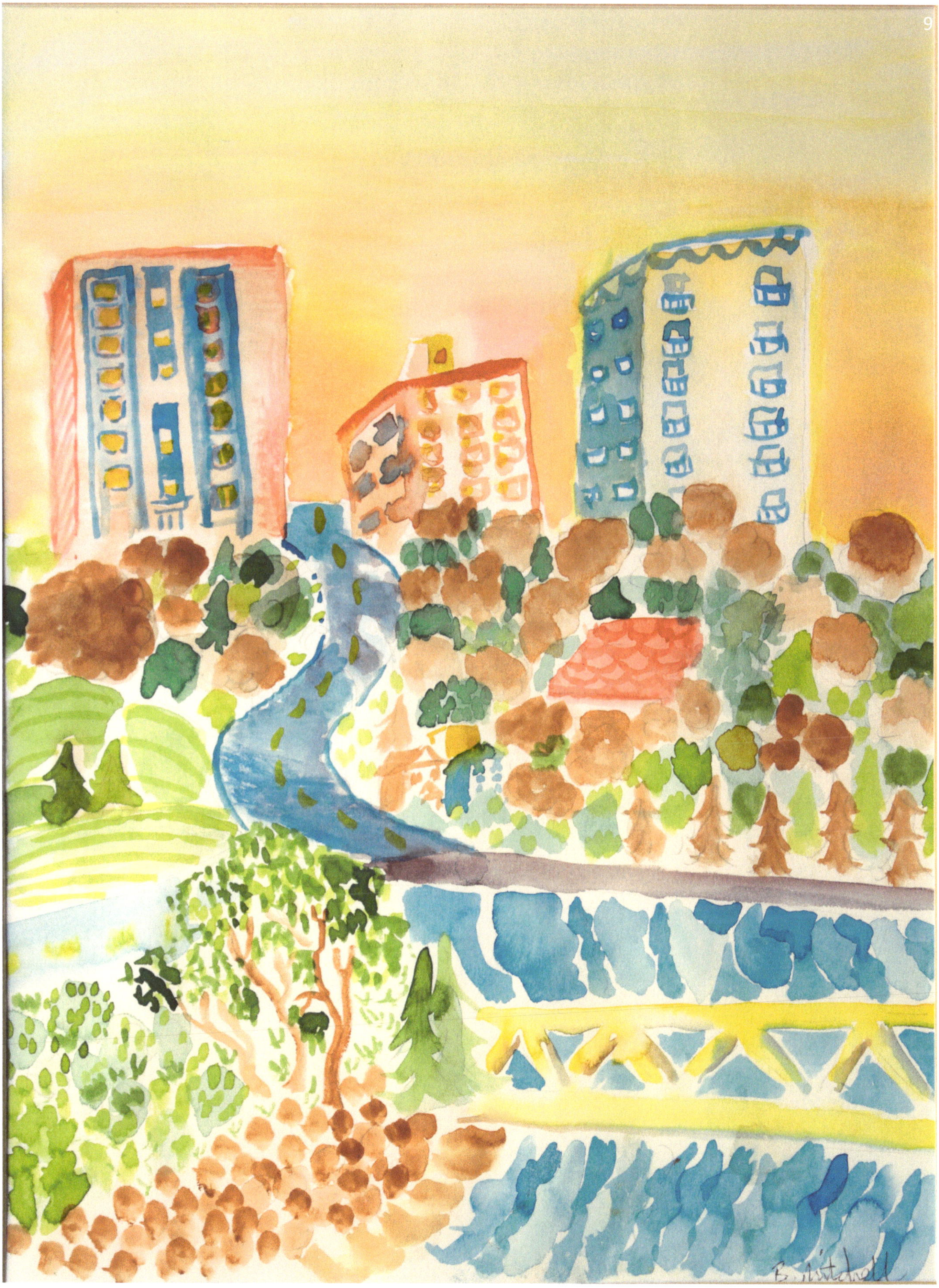

Whyte and Fourth, ca.2011. Watercolour

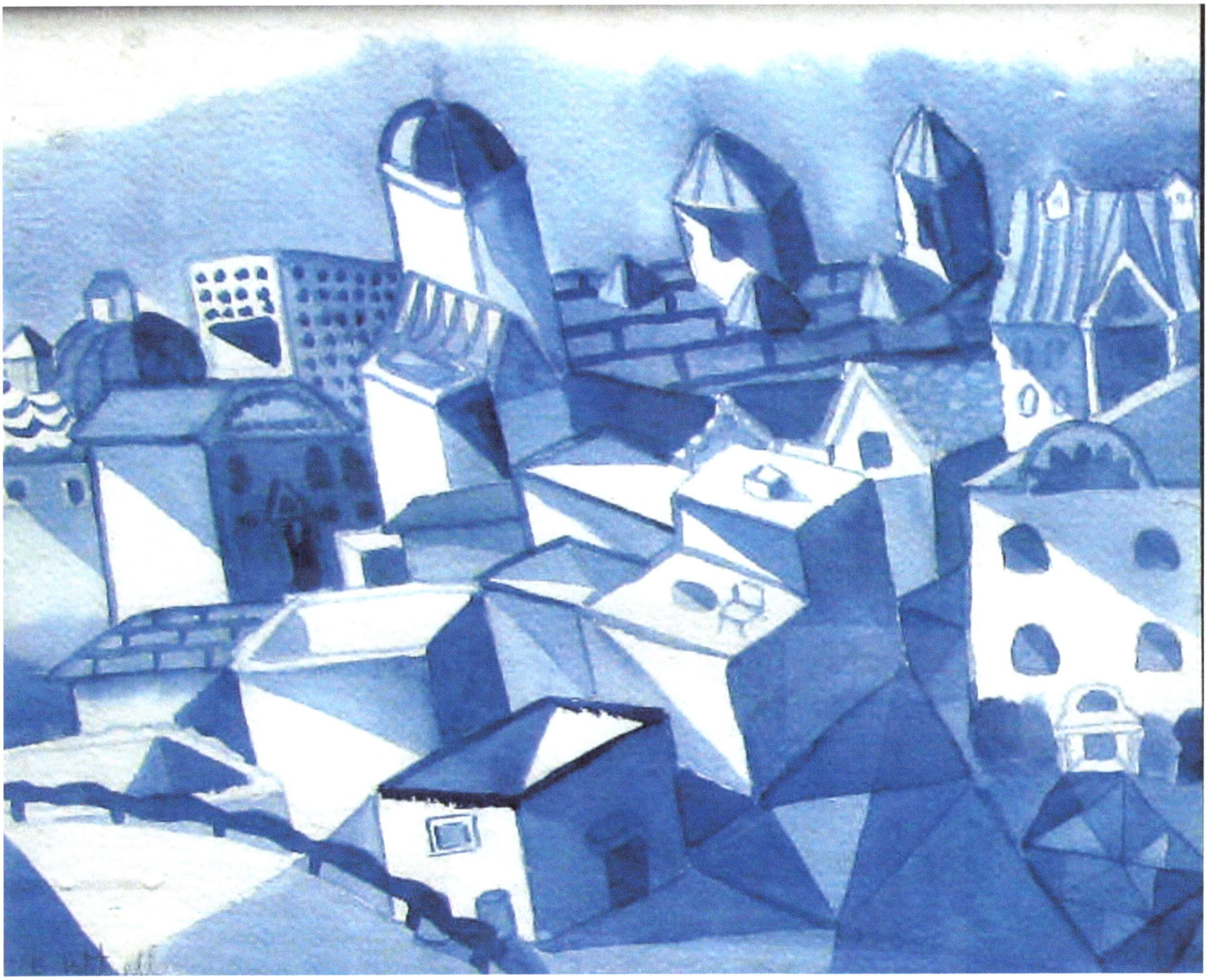

Sunrise in St. Albert, ca. 2011. Watercolour

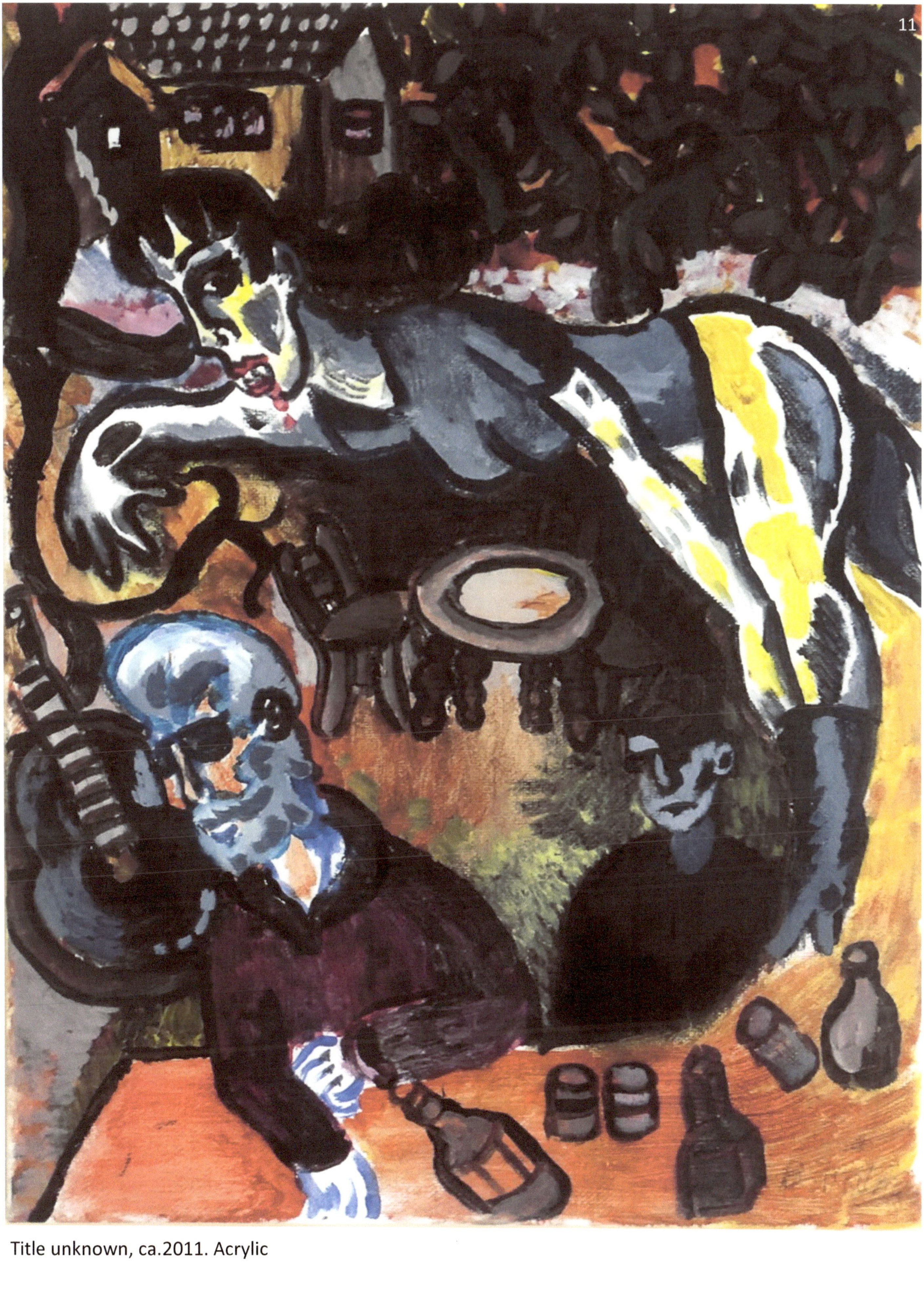

Title unknown, ca.2011. Acrylic

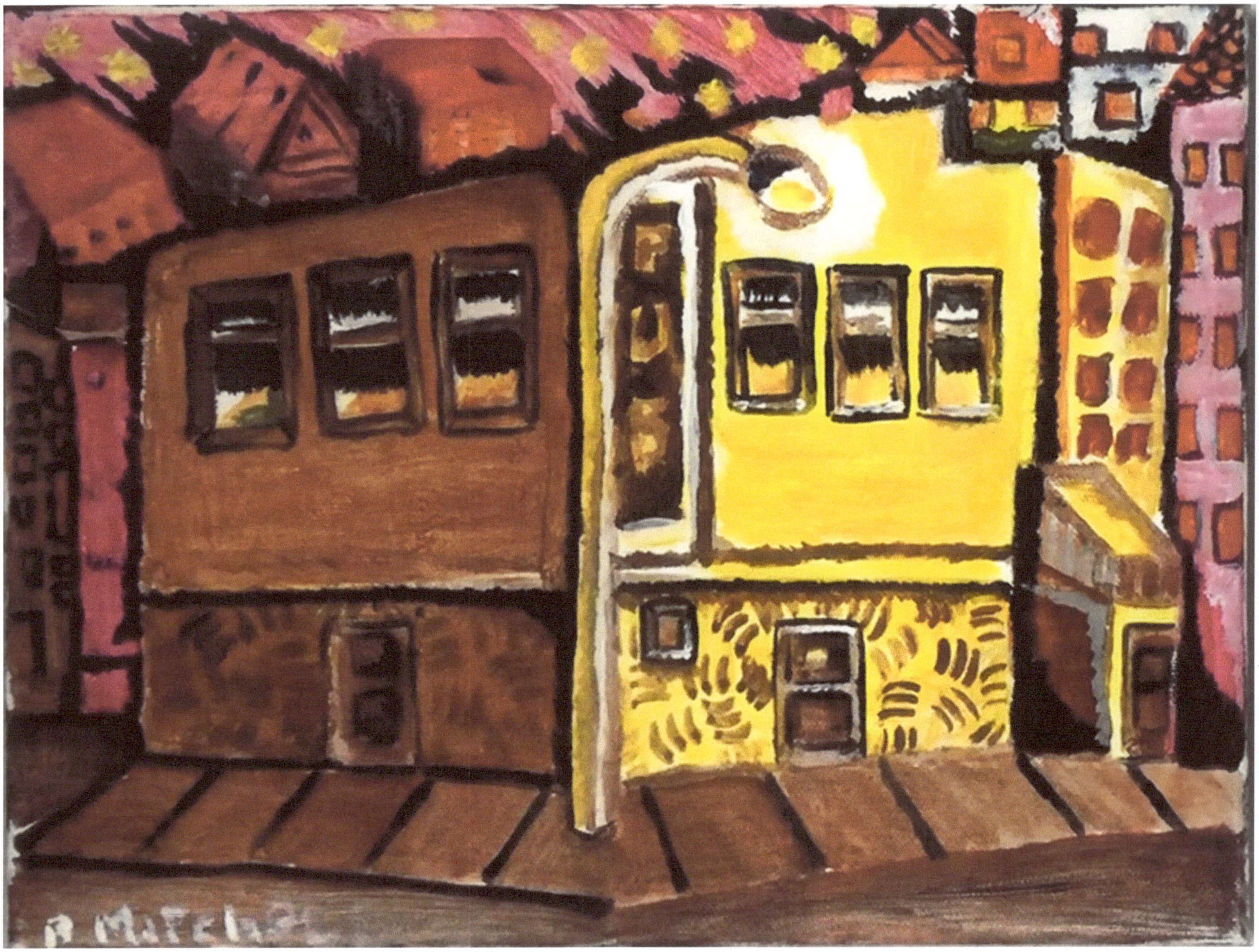

Title unknown, 2013. Acrylic

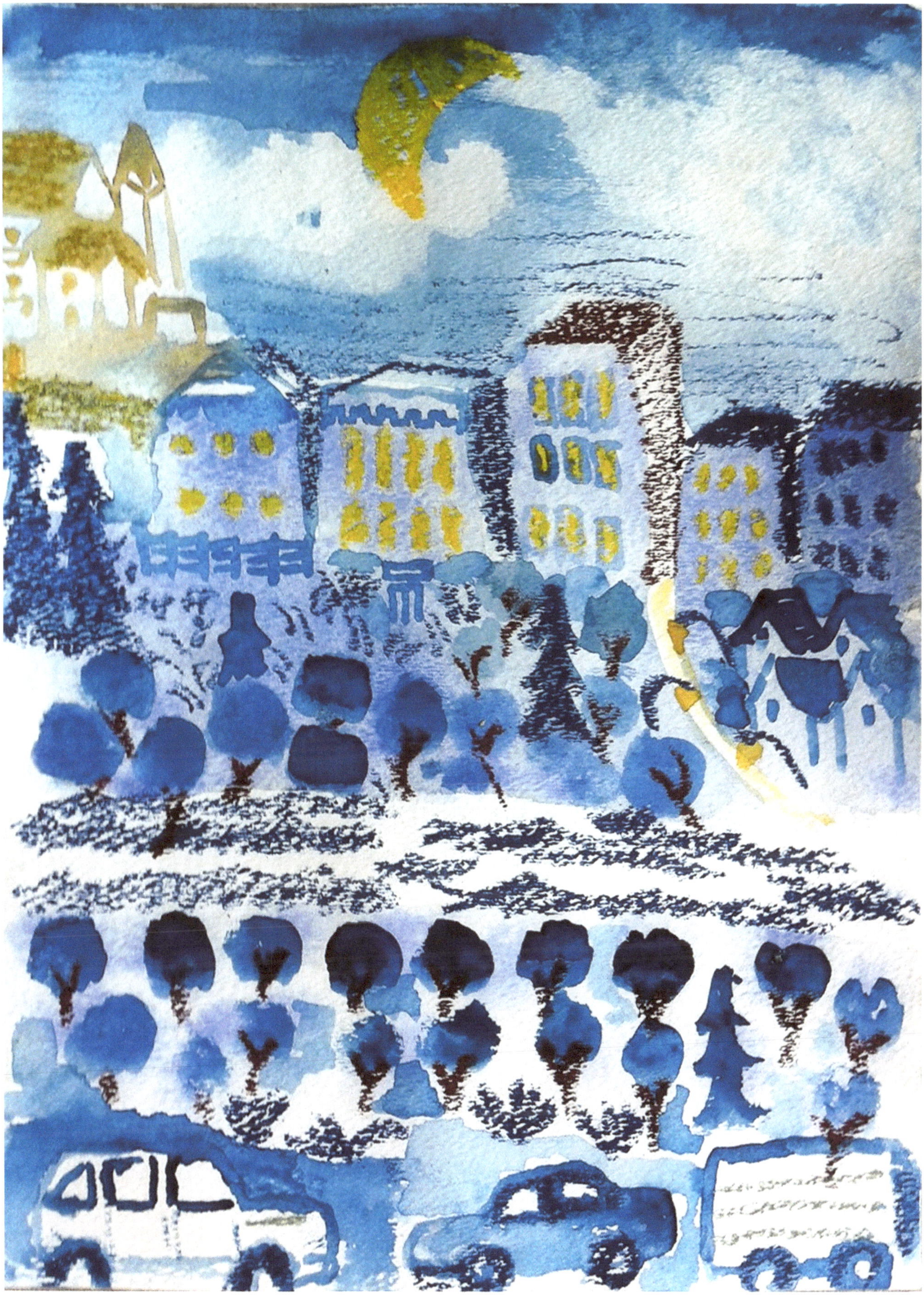

Title unknown, ca.2013. Watercolour

Painting used as poster for an art show at the Nina Hagerty Centre

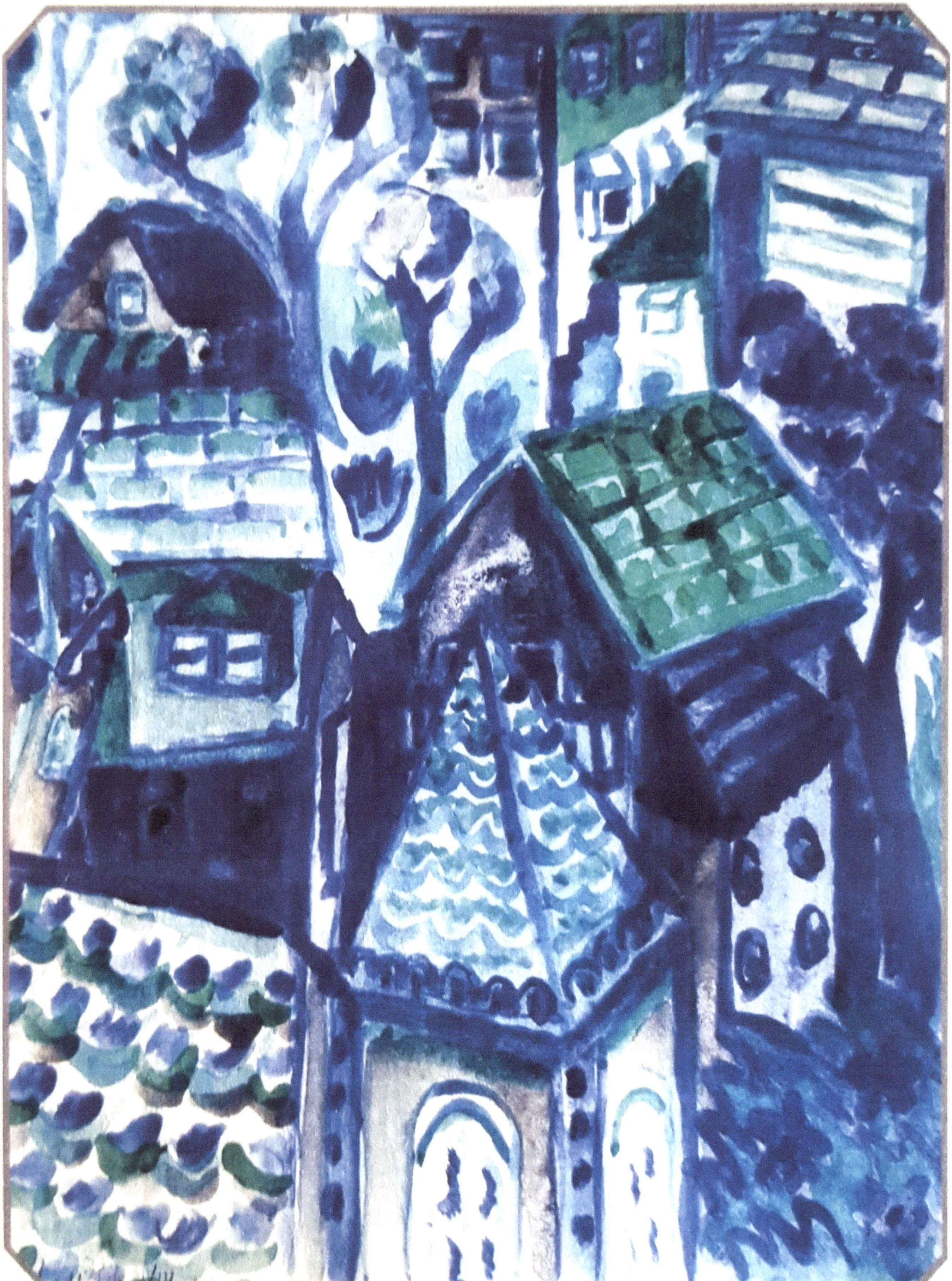

Title unknown, ca.2014. Watercolour

Painting used by Rachel Notley for the Christmas card in her riding

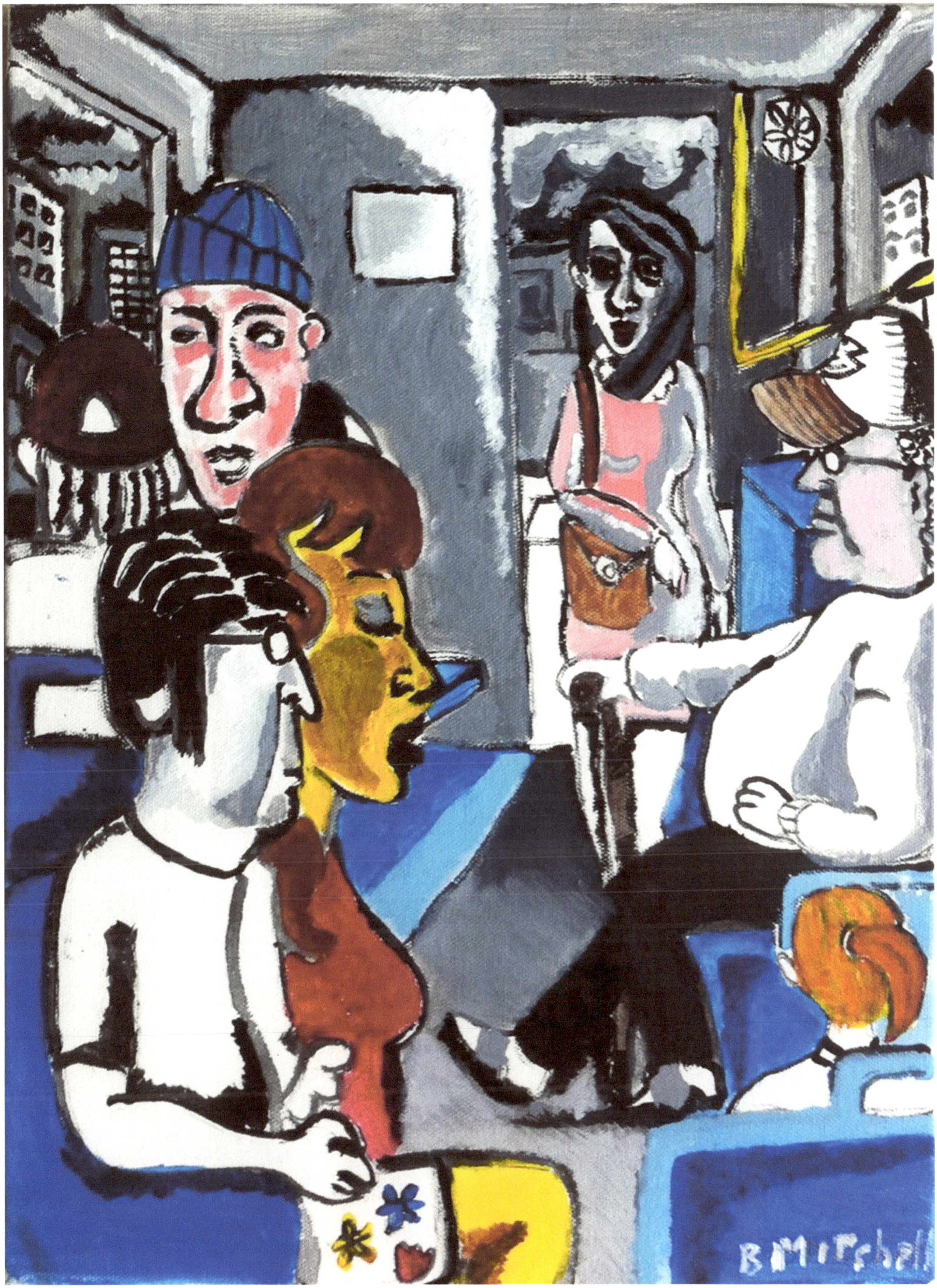

Title unknown, ca.2013. Acrylic

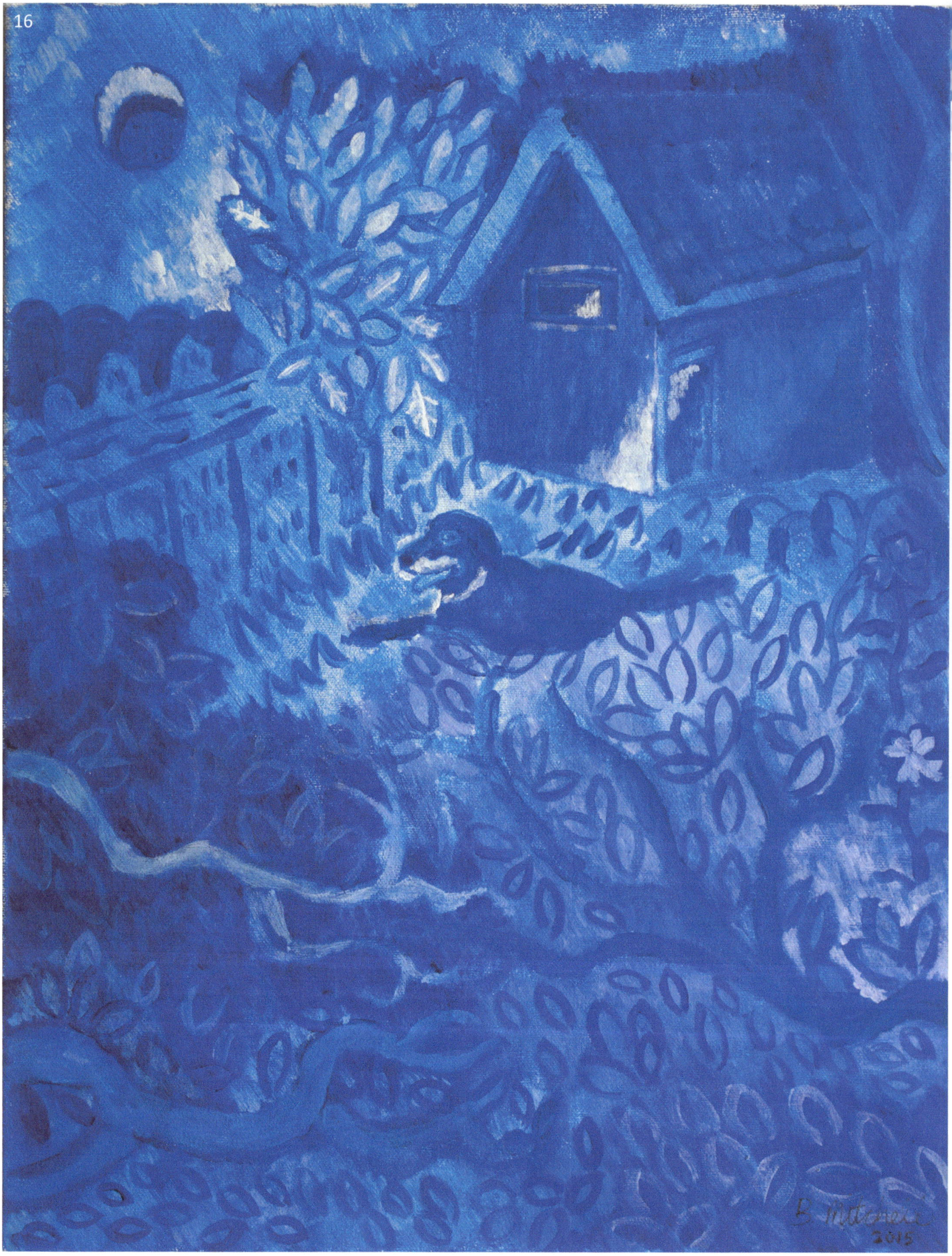

Untitled painting of Walker, 2015. Acrylic on canvas

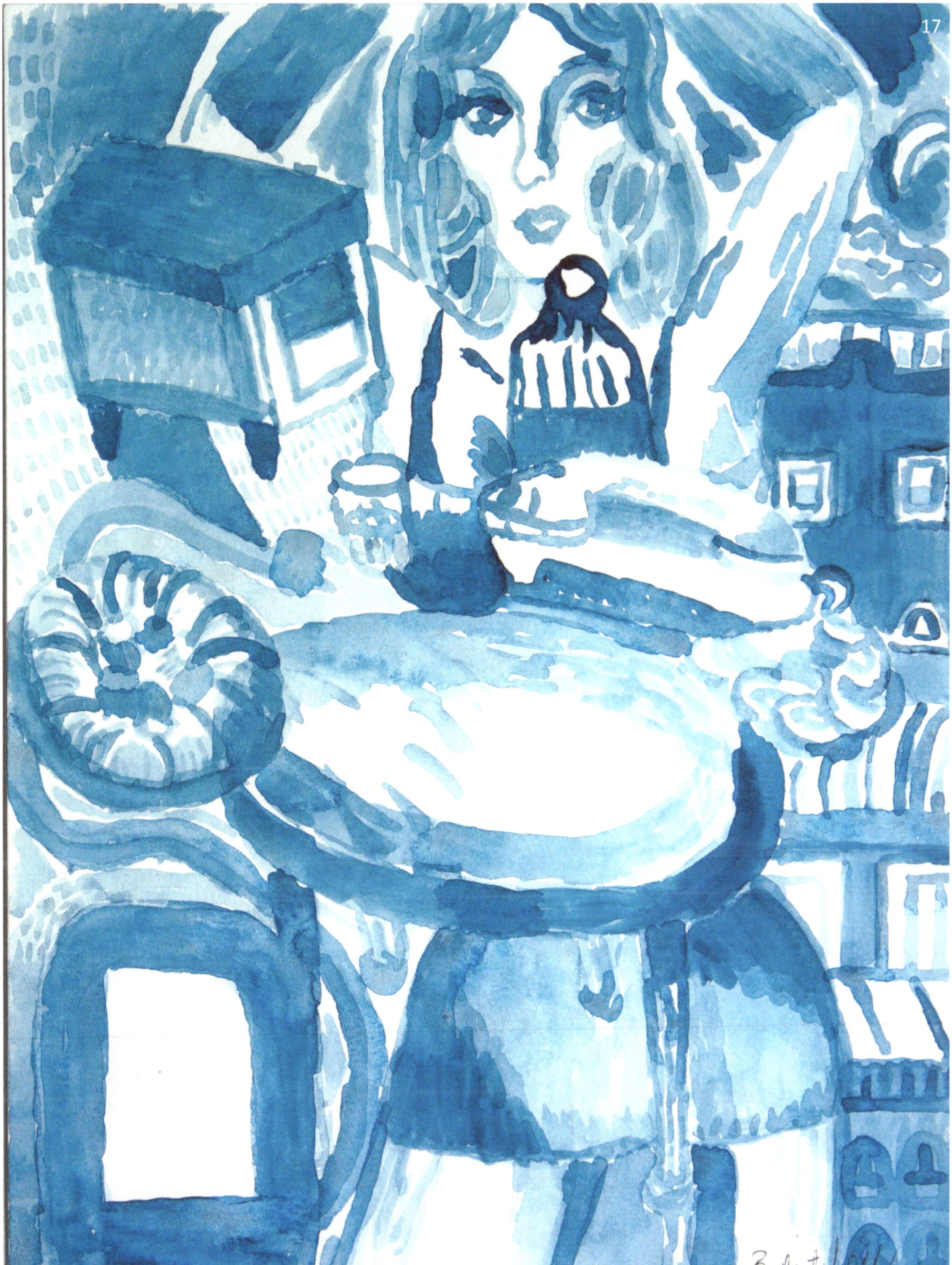

The Hotel Motel, 2015. Watercolour

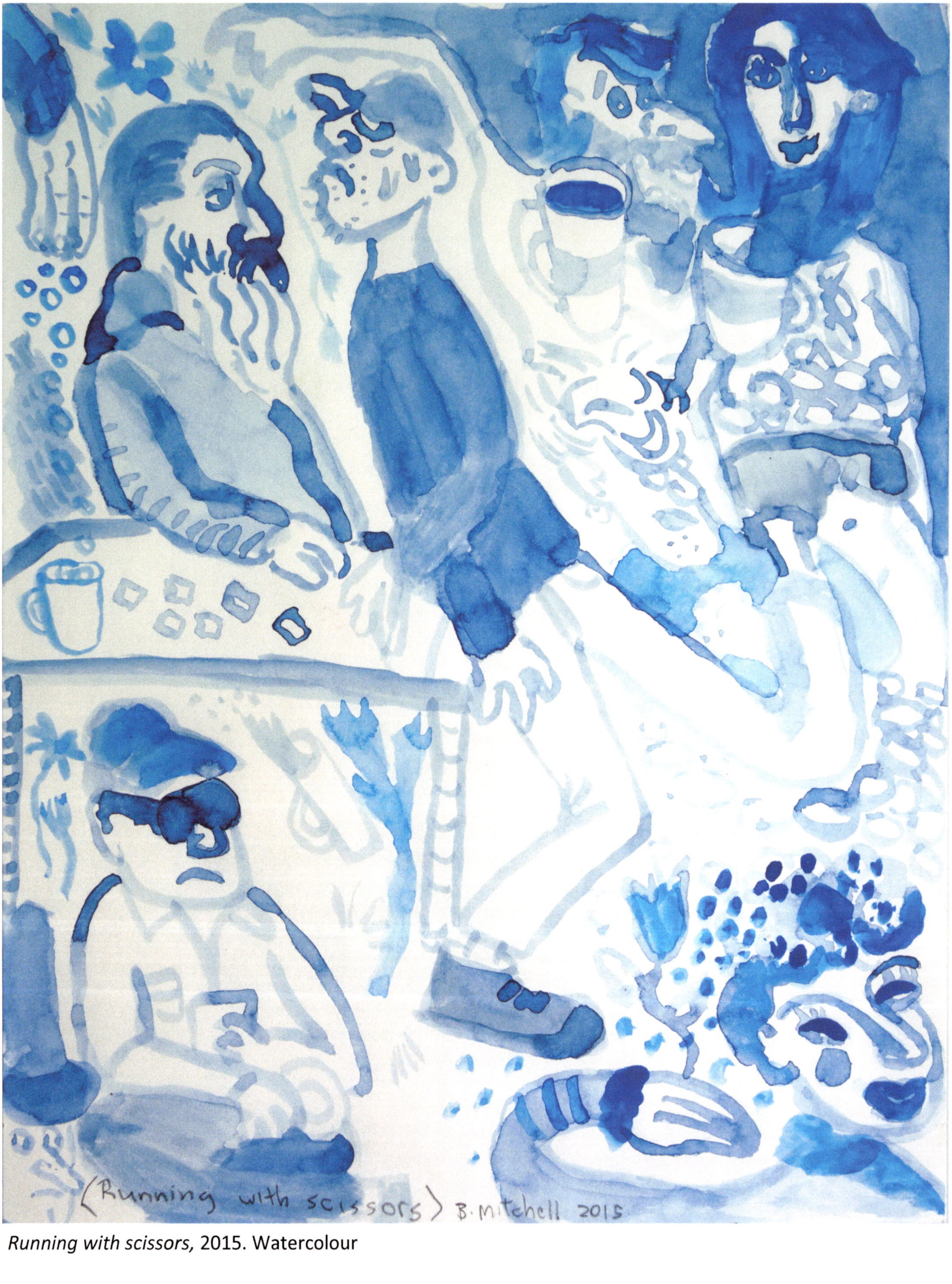

Running with scissors, 2015. Watercolour

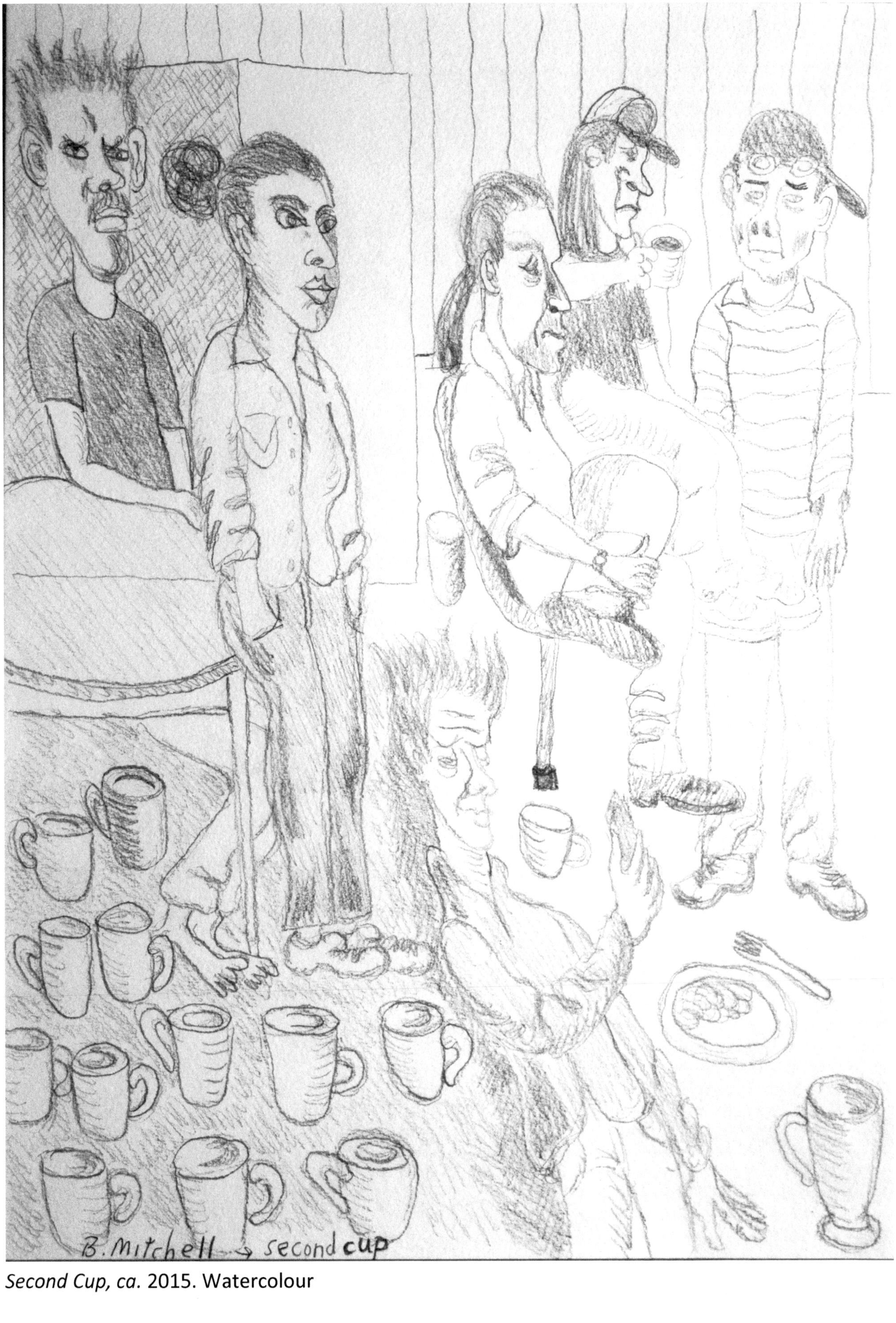

Second Cup, ca. 2015. Watercolour

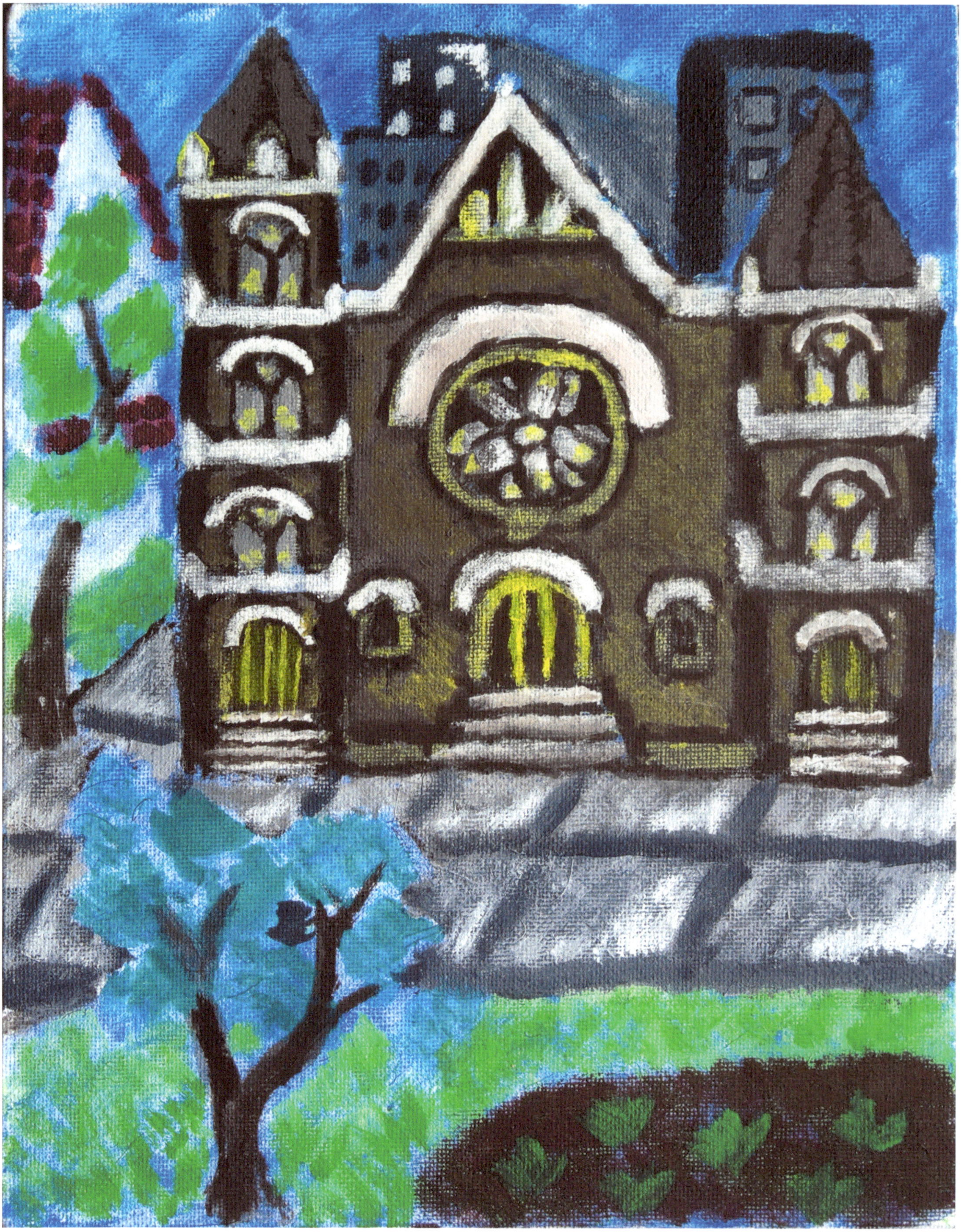

Sacred Heart, ca. 2016. Acrylic on Canvas

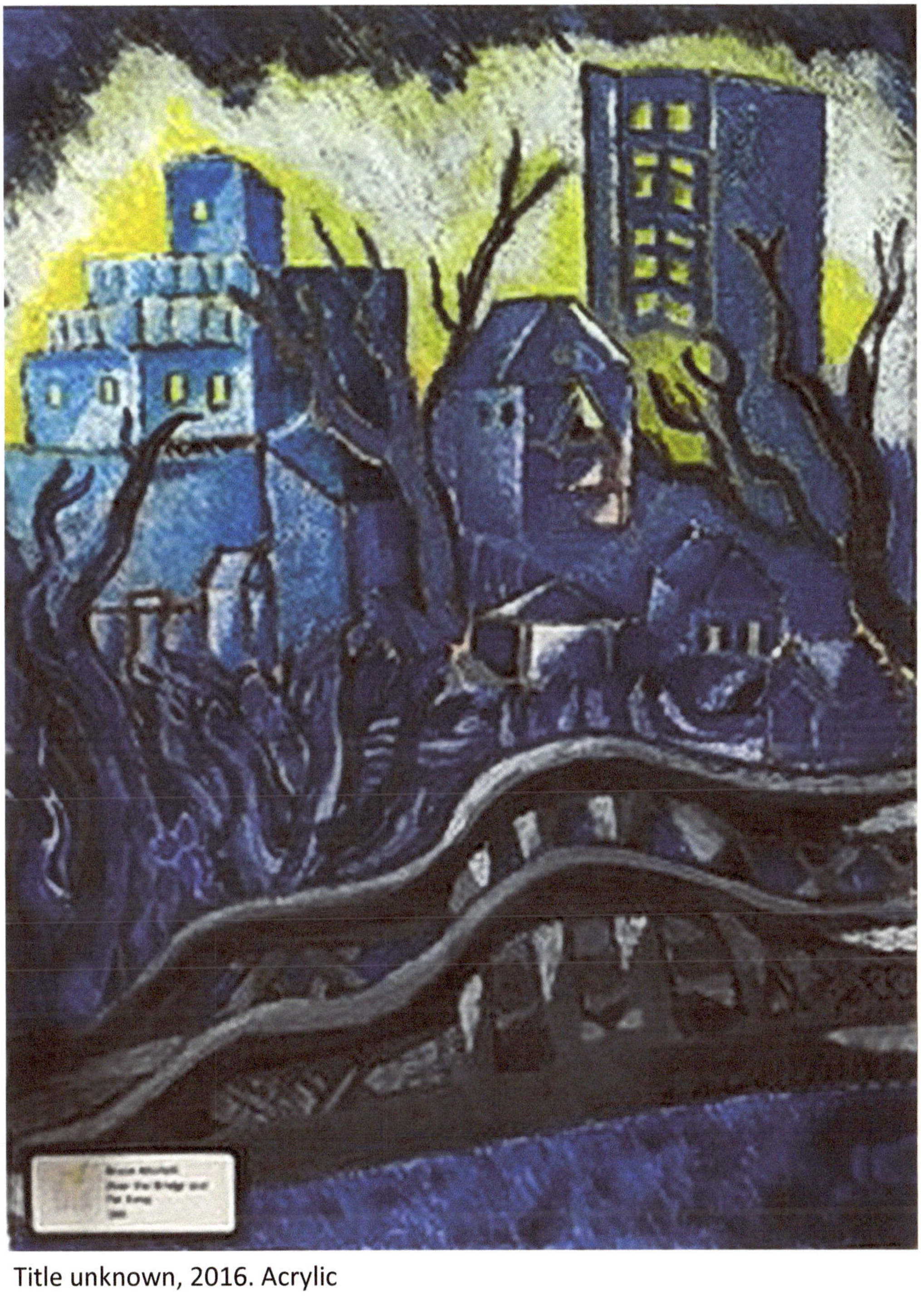

Title unknown, 2016. Acrylic

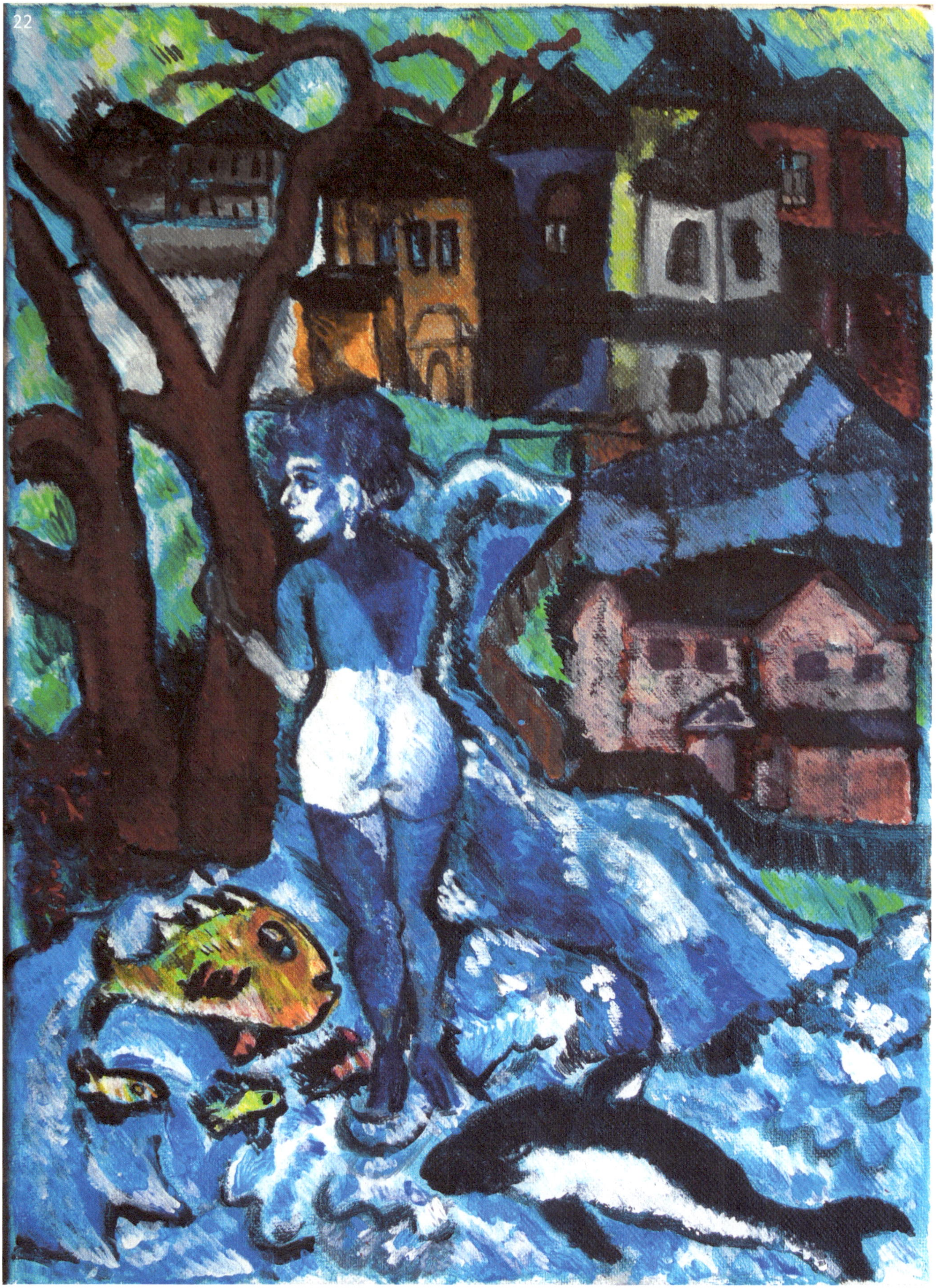

Title unknown, 2017. Acrylic on canvas

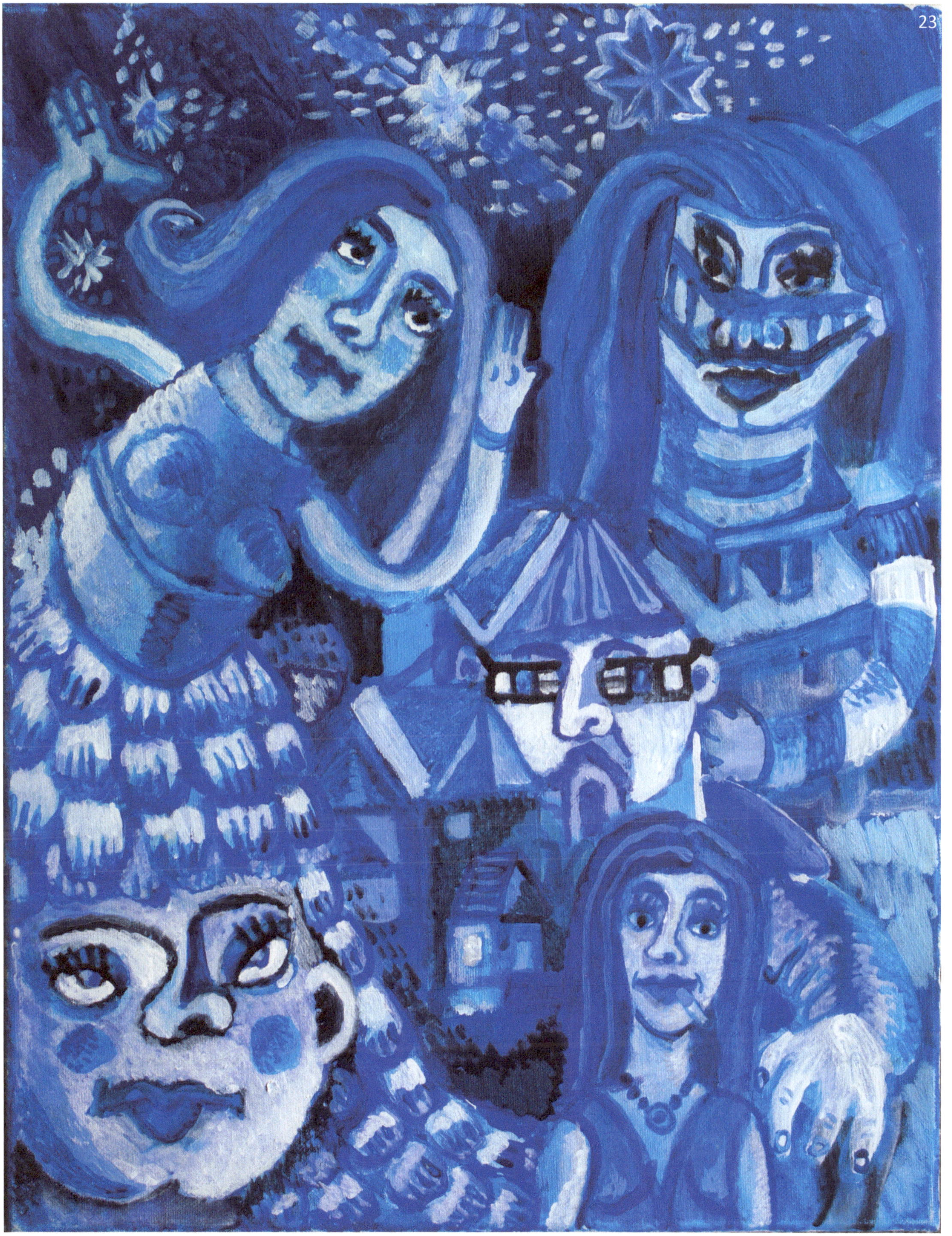

Carnival on my street, 2017. Acrylic on canvas

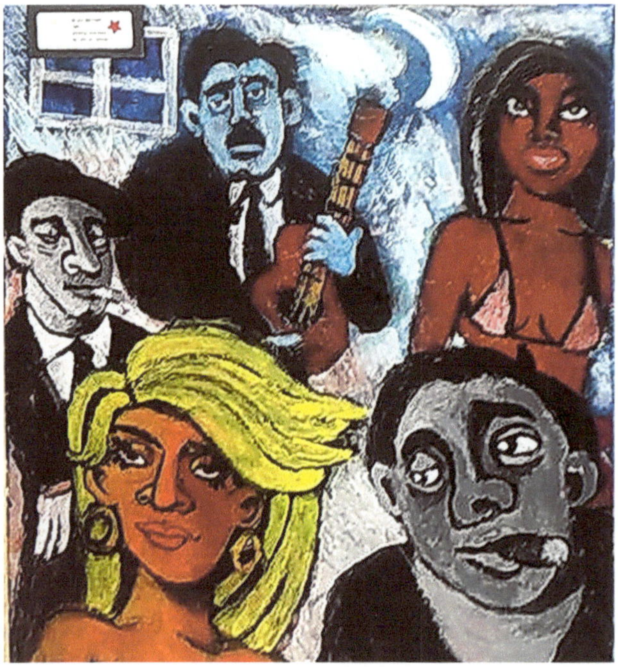

Top, *Anthony Scarboni* , 2017. Acrylic

Cropped version of original painting

Bottom, *Borden park,* ca. 2018. Acrylic

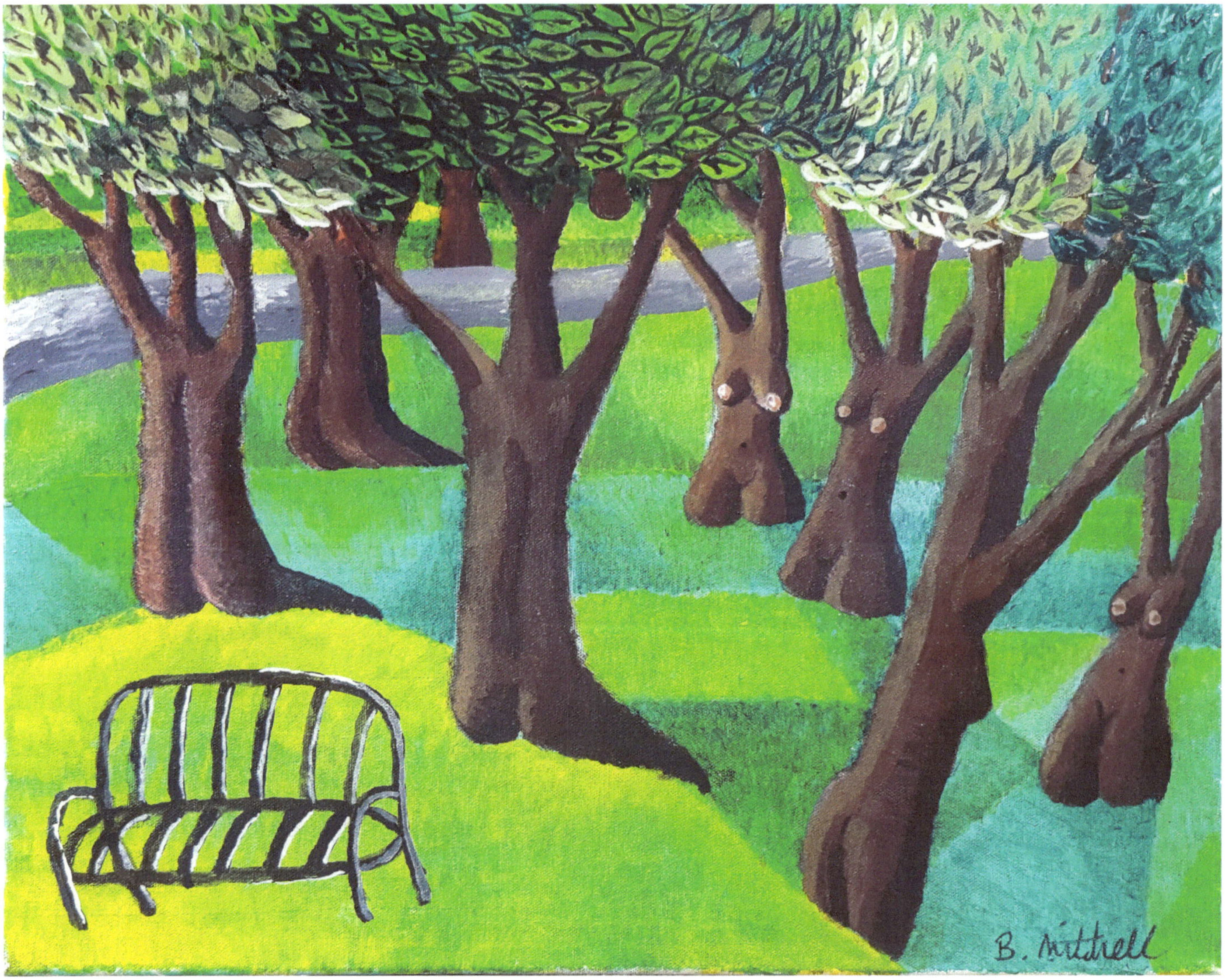

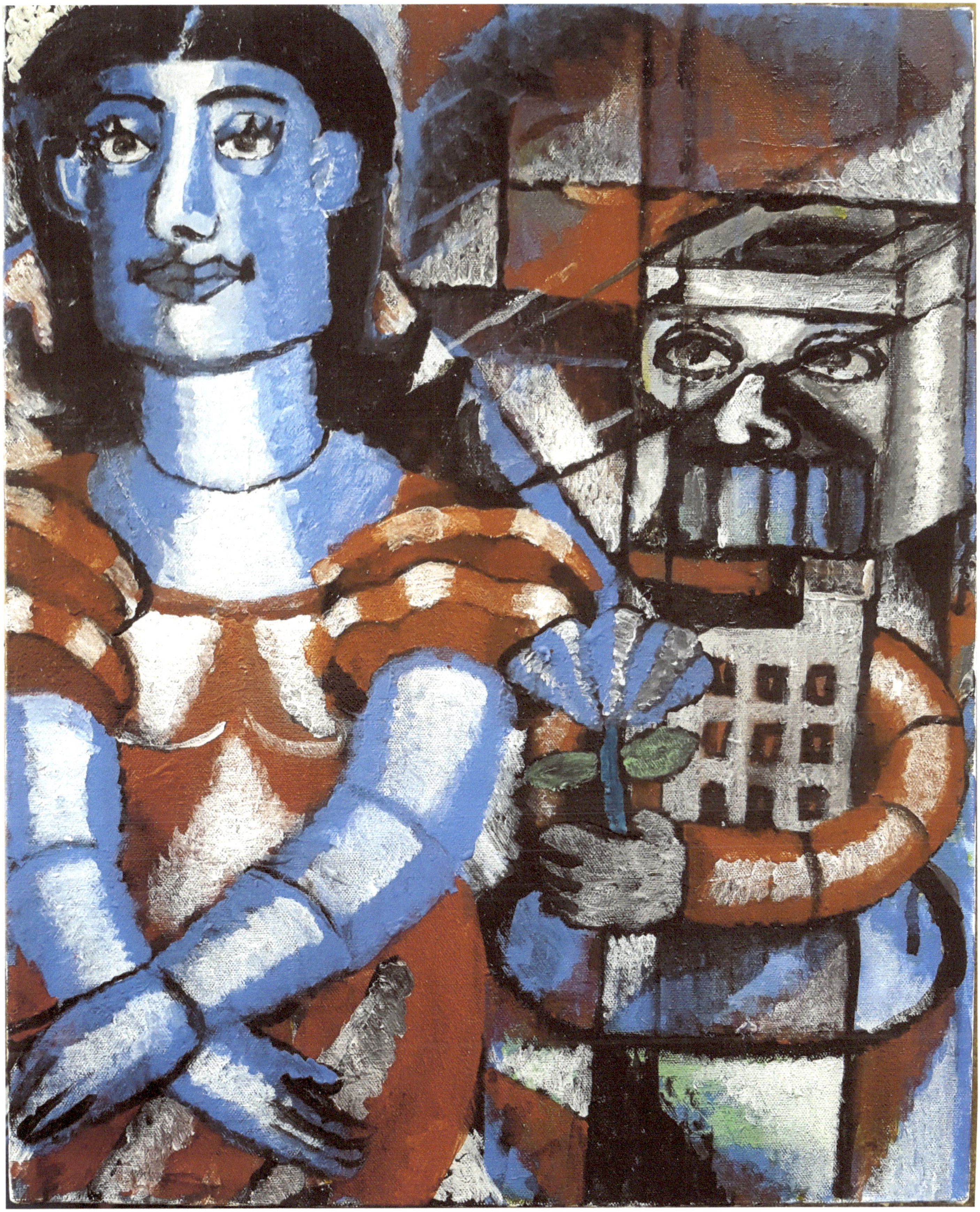

Title unknown, ca. 2018. Acrylic

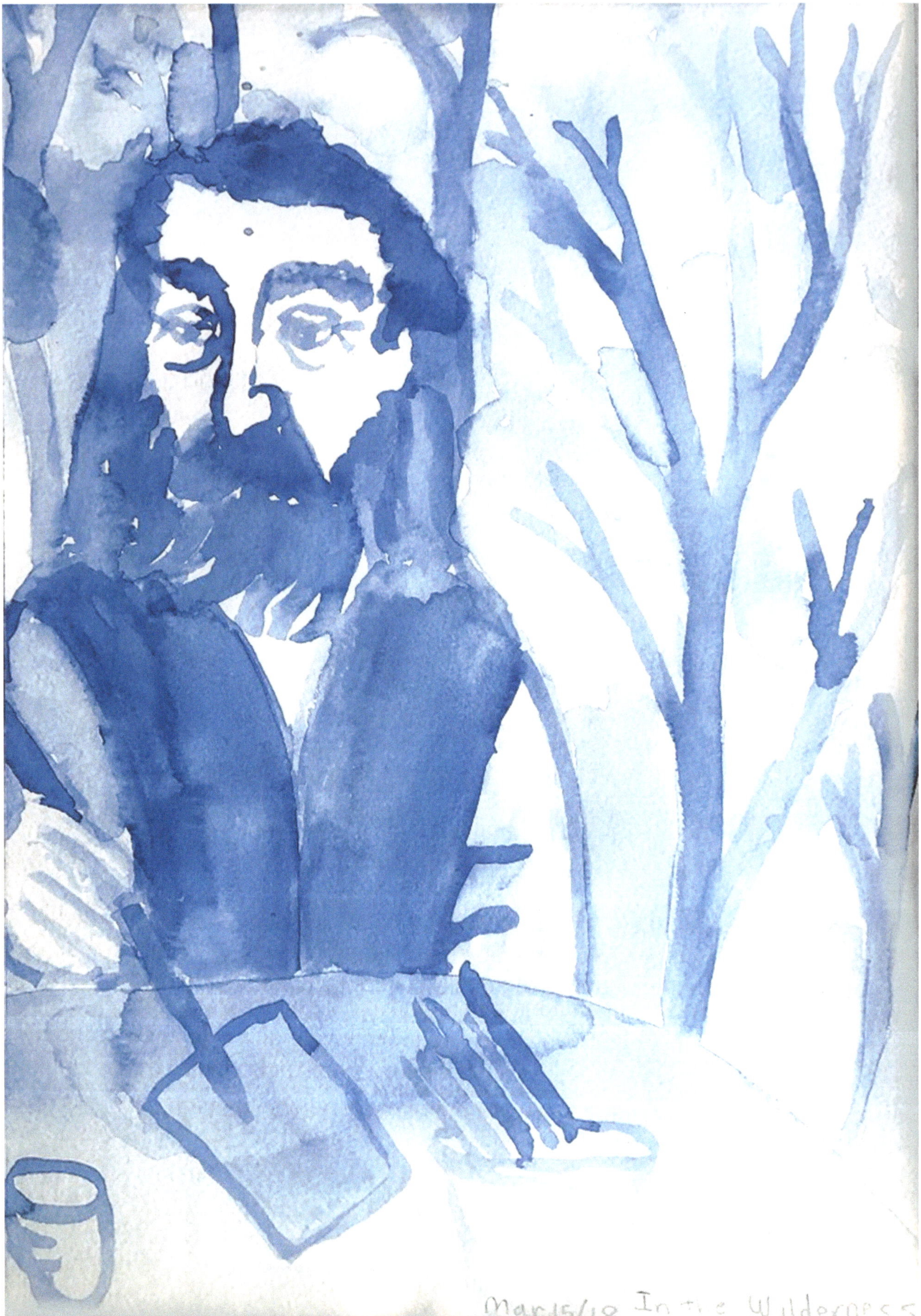

In the Wilderness, 2018. Acrylic

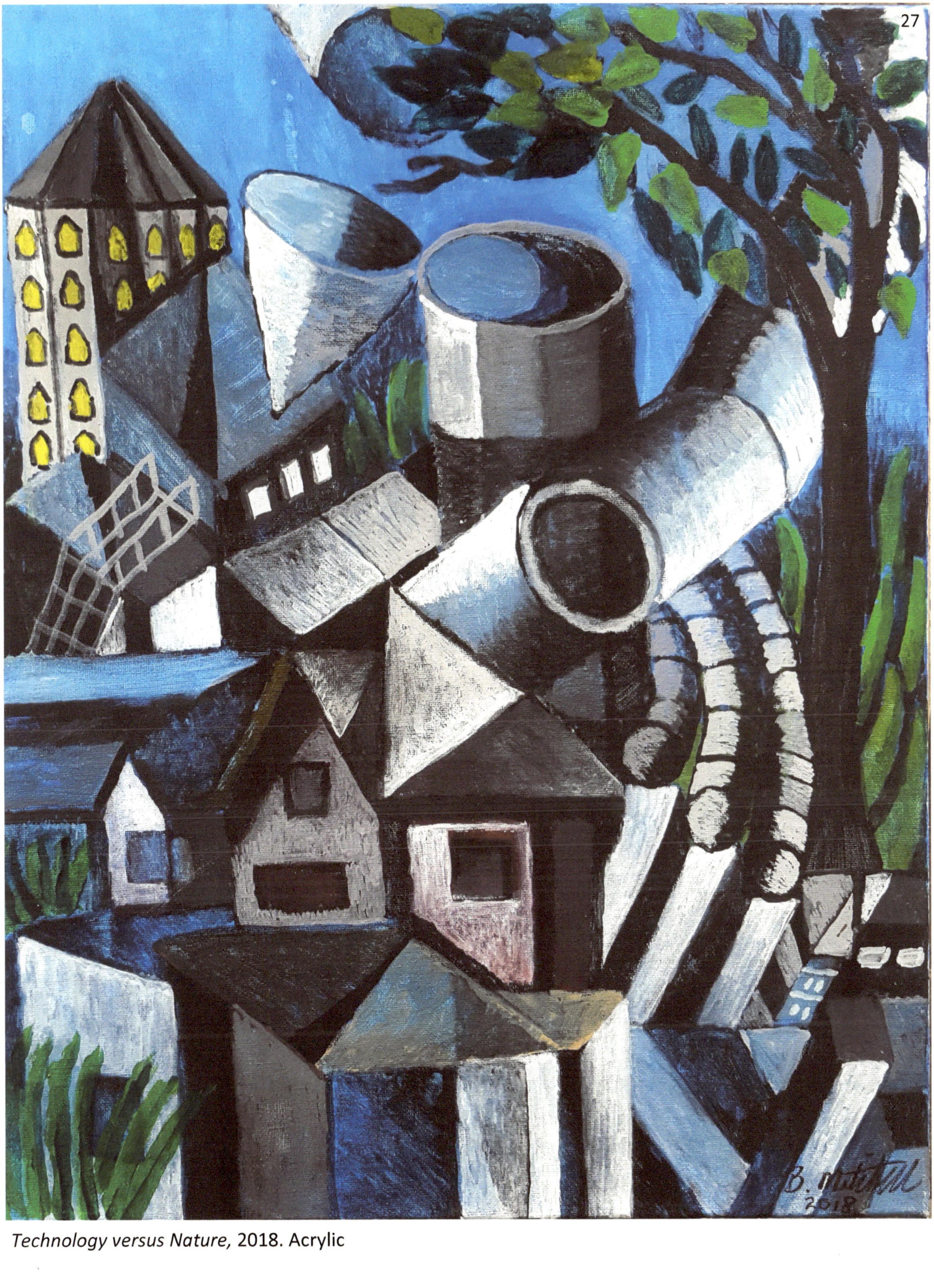

Technology versus Nature, 2018. Acrylic

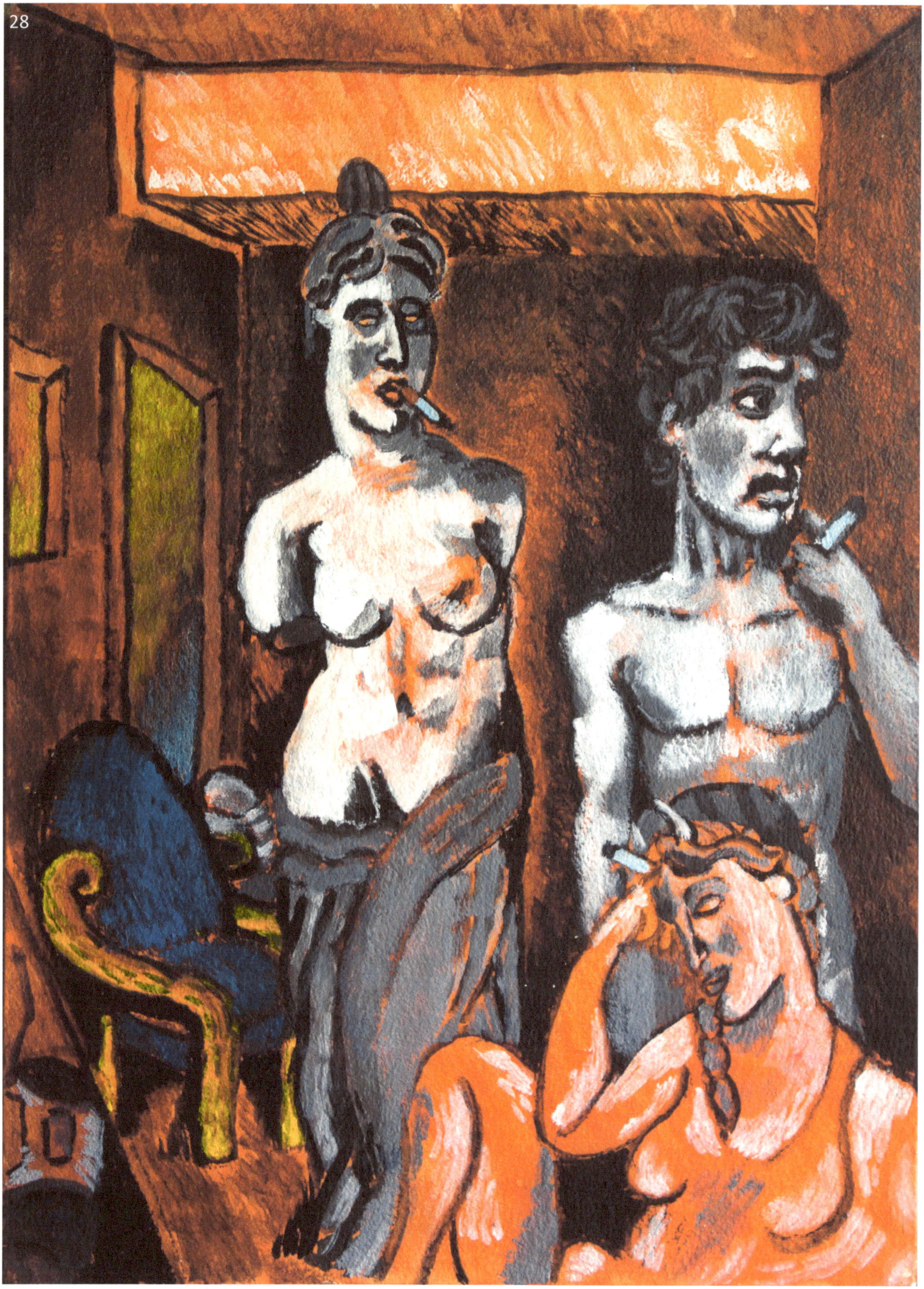

Unsigned painting depicts Greek statues in therapy, ca. 2018. Acrylic on canvas

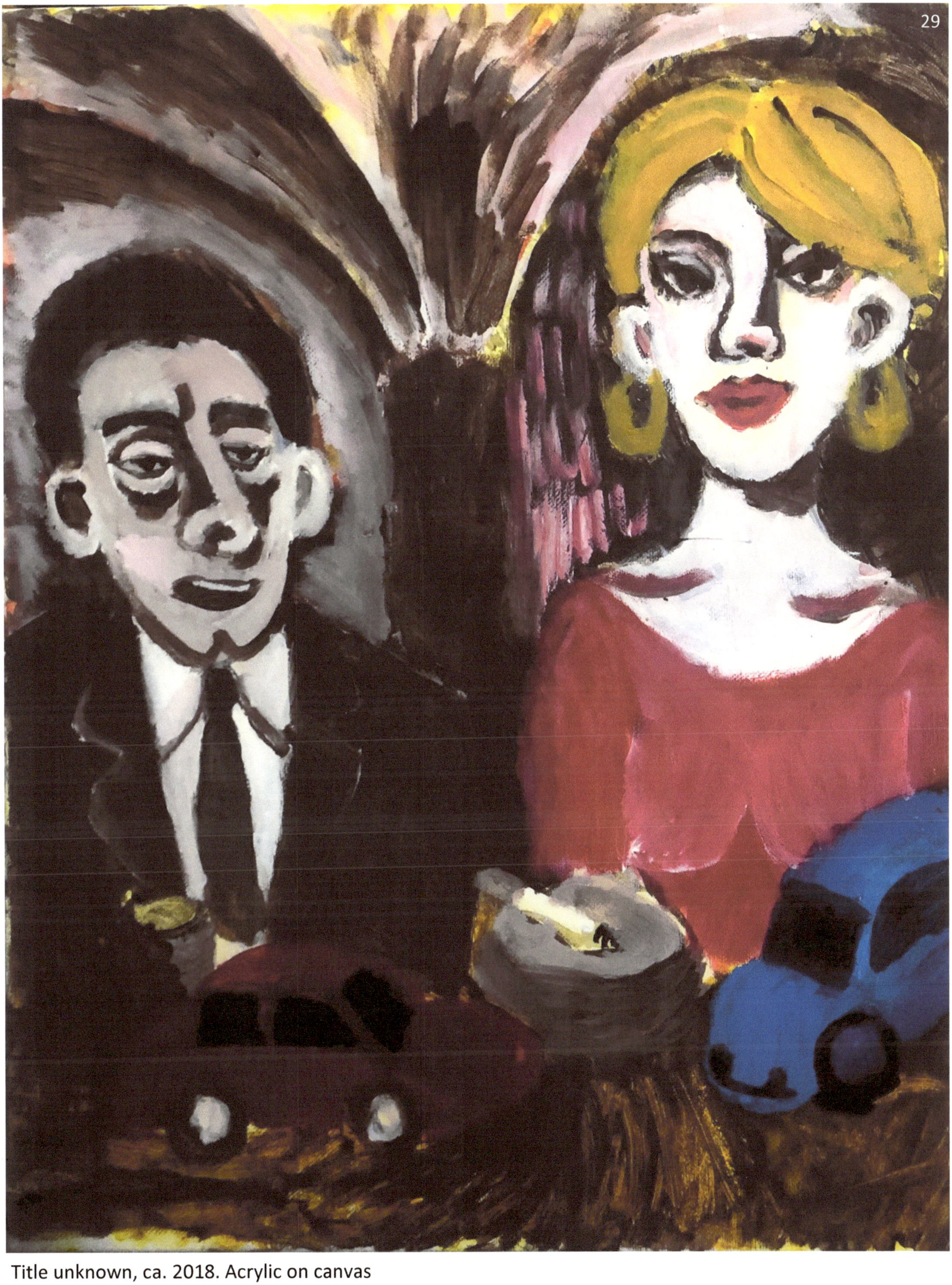

Title unknown, ca. 2018. Acrylic on canvas

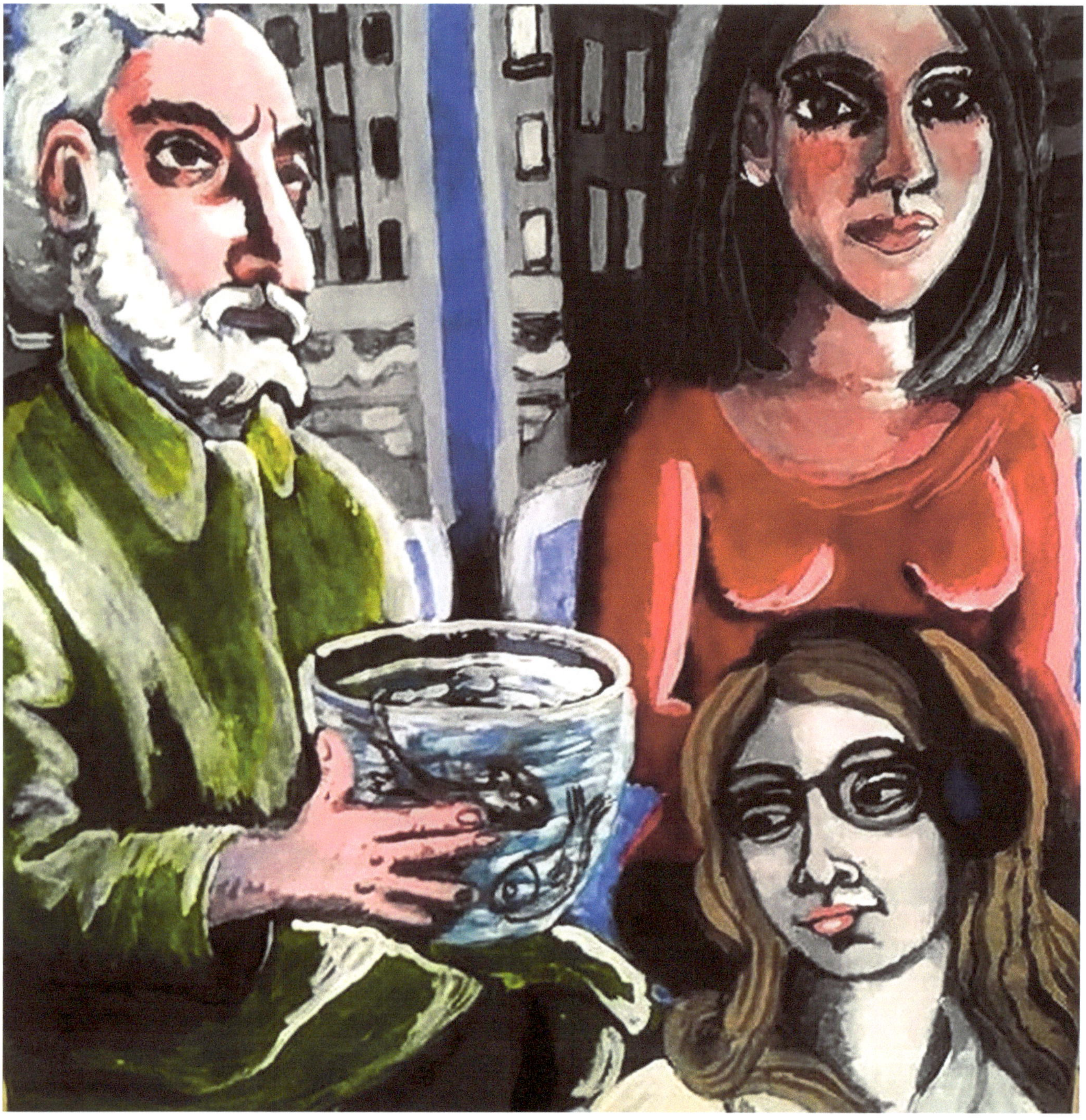

Noah on the Bus. 2018. Acrylic on canvas
Cropped version of original painting

"I am calling it Noah on the bus. Noah is wearing a raincoat and is going to be holding a bowl of fish. It's a theme of modern day prophets"
B. Mitchell, November, 2018.

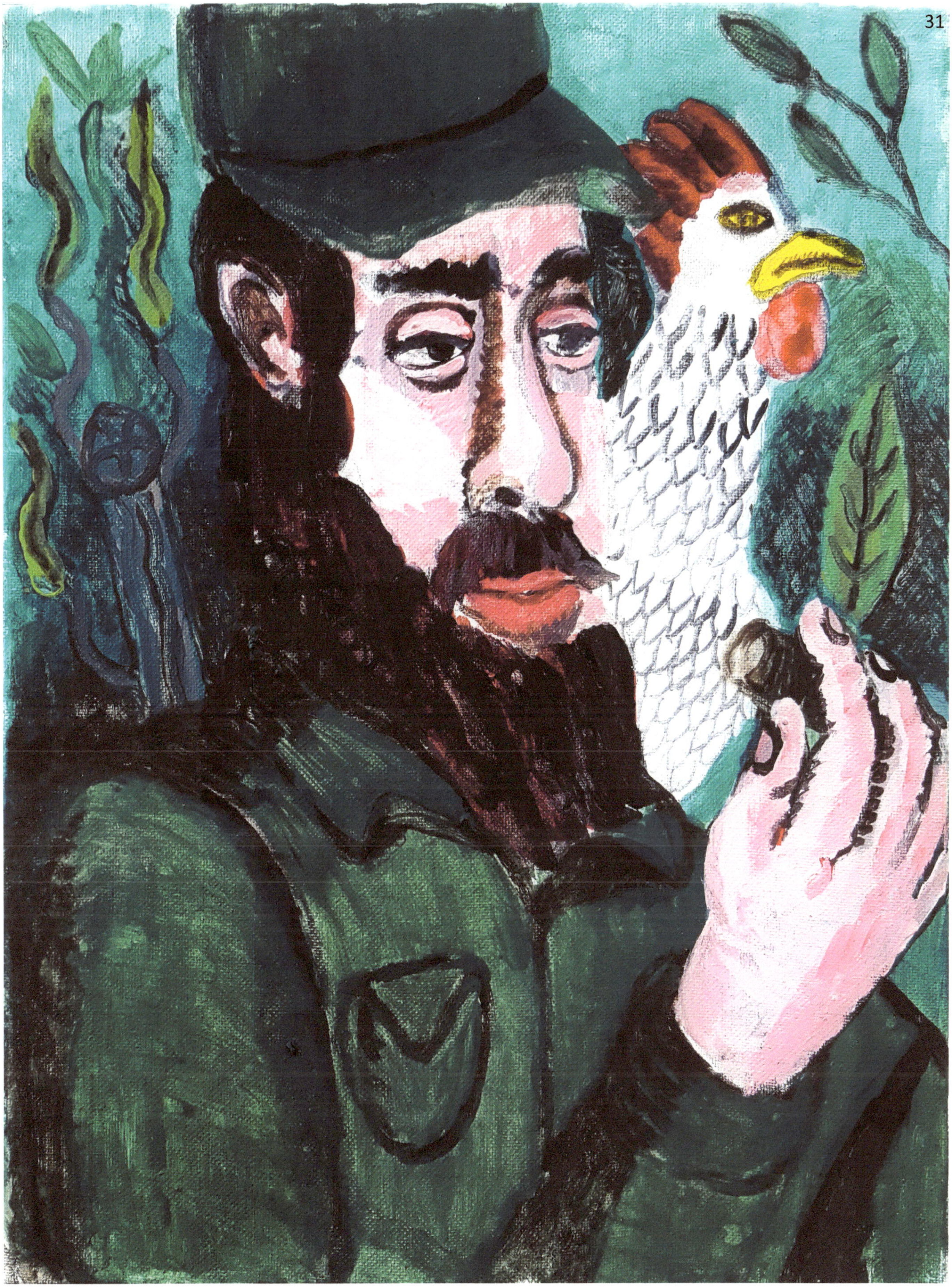

Title unknown, ca. 2018. Acrylic on canvas

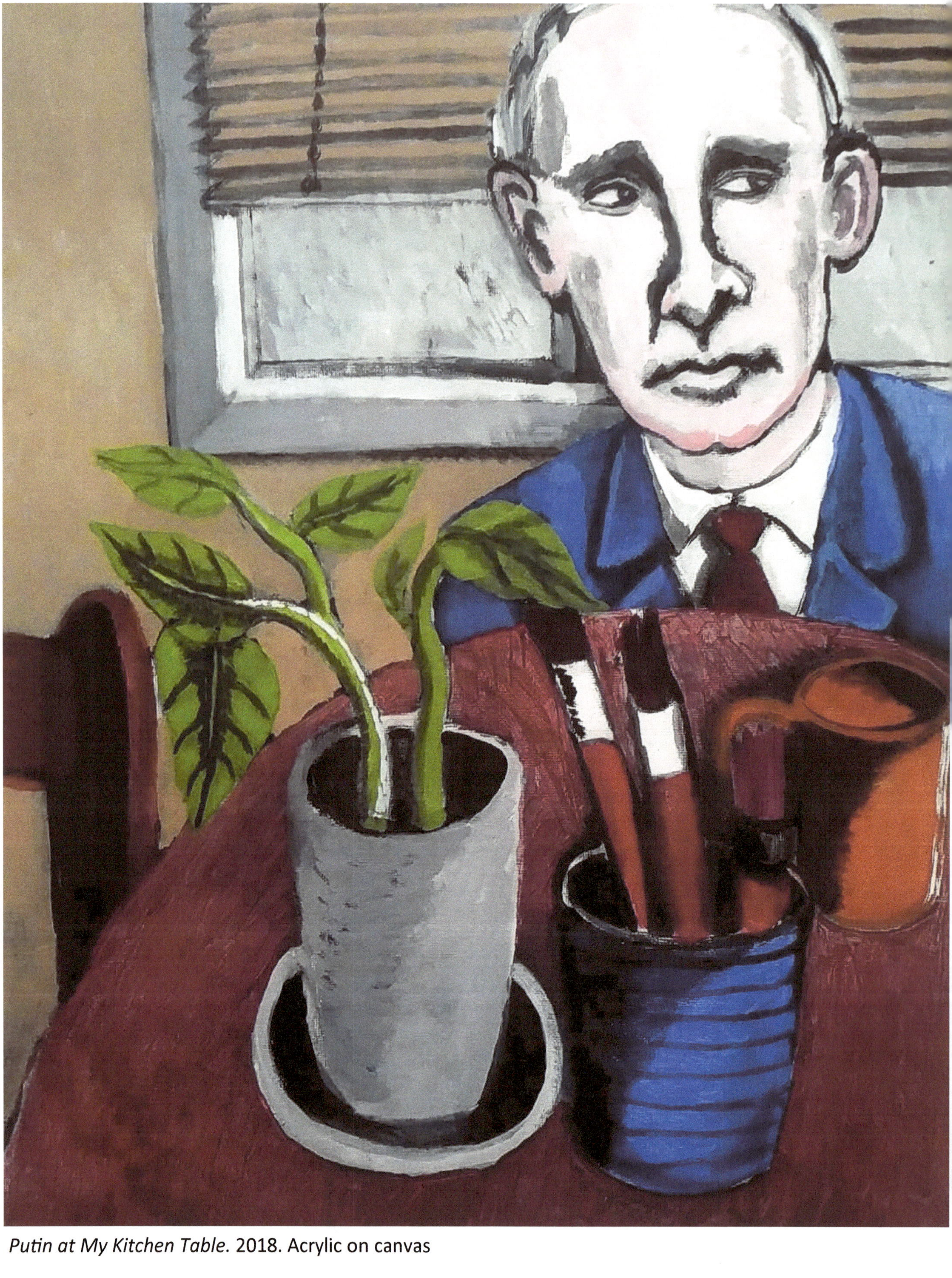

Putin at My Kitchen Table. 2018. Acrylic on canvas

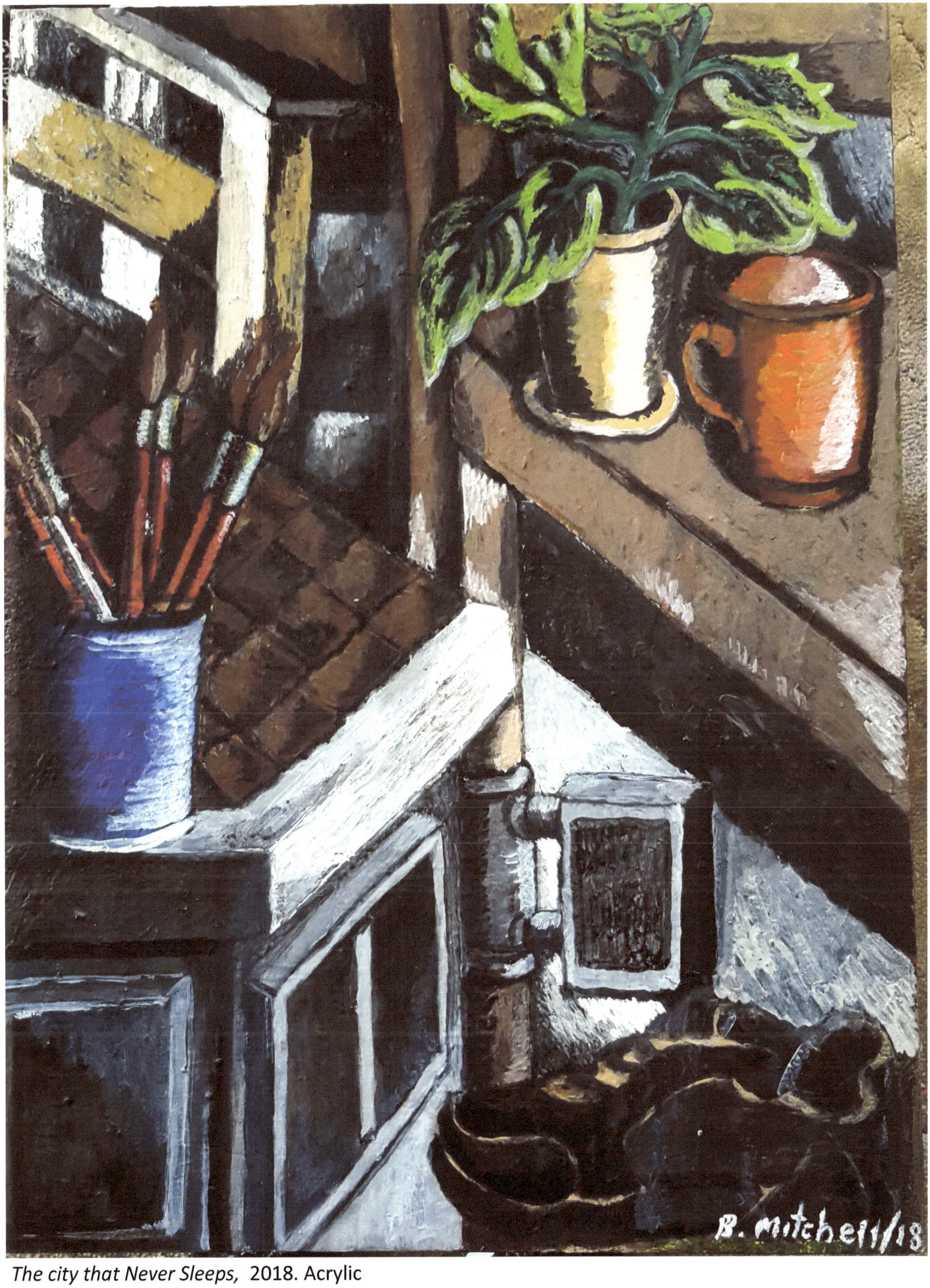

The city that Never Sleeps, 2018. Acrylic

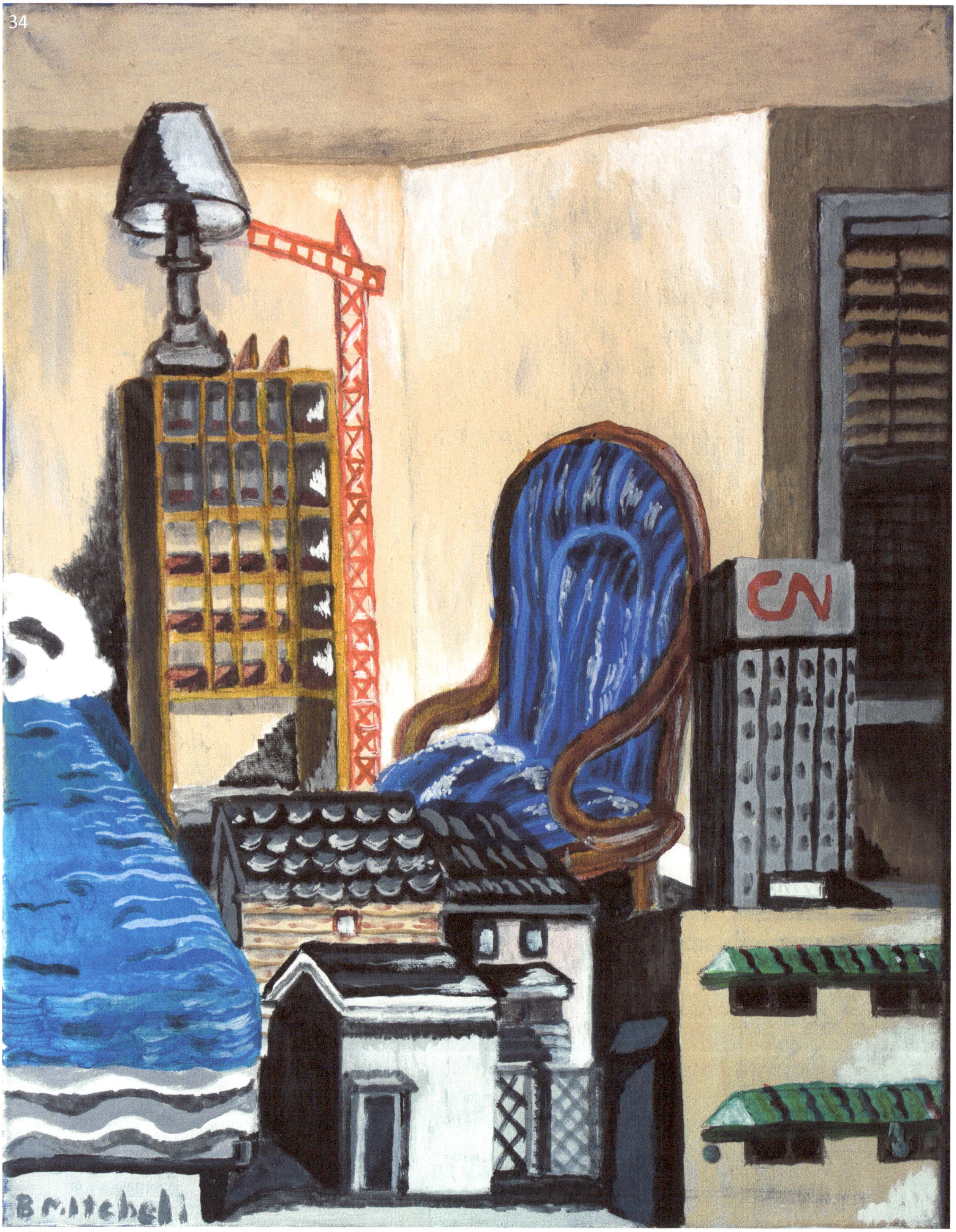

Downtown in my bedroom, 2018. Acrylic

"A story about living downtown. It (is) hard to detach yourself from the city even when you close the door on your apartment" B. Mitchell Dec. 2018

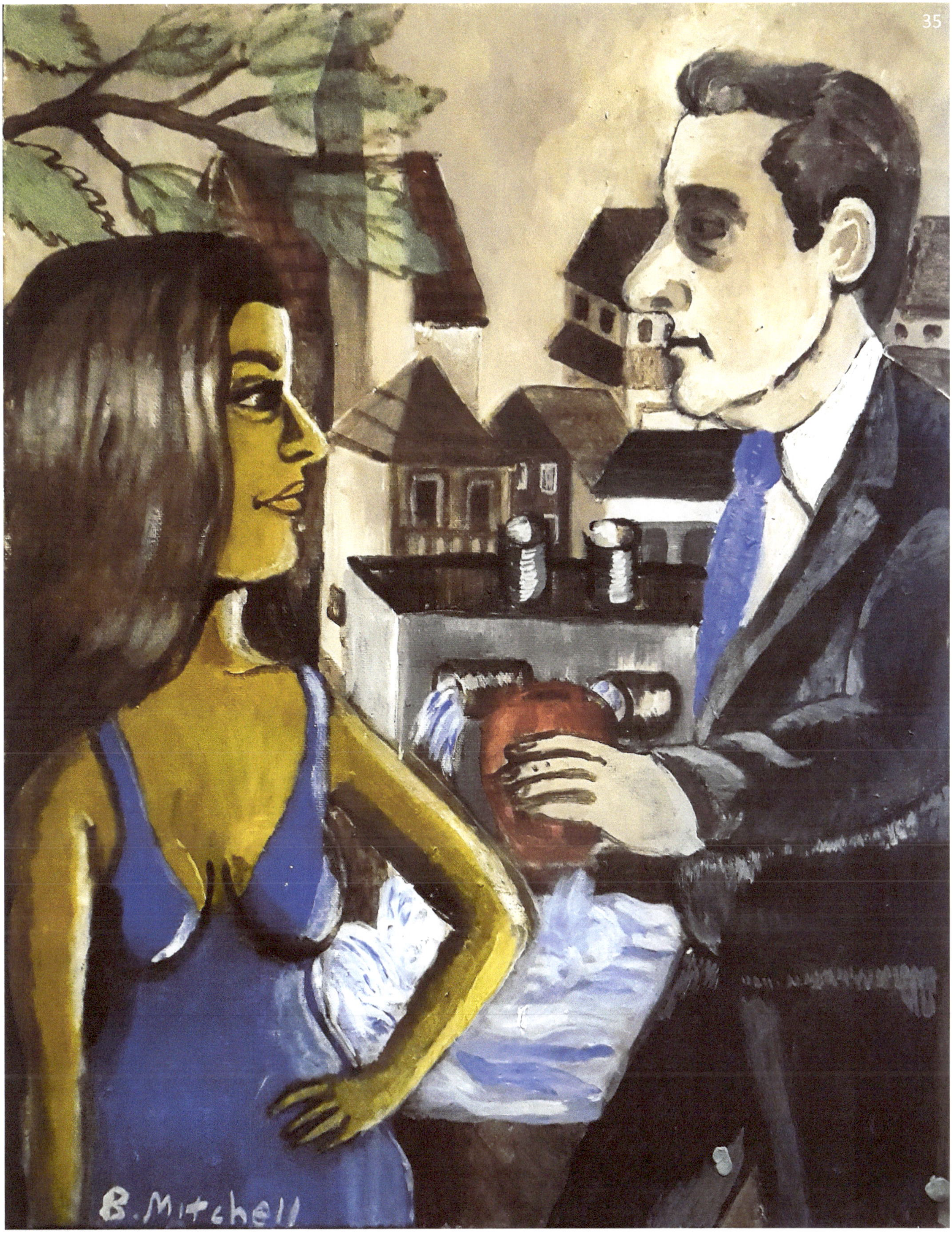

Grace 2, 2019. Acrylic

"A modernized version of Adam and eve" B. Mitchell January, 2019

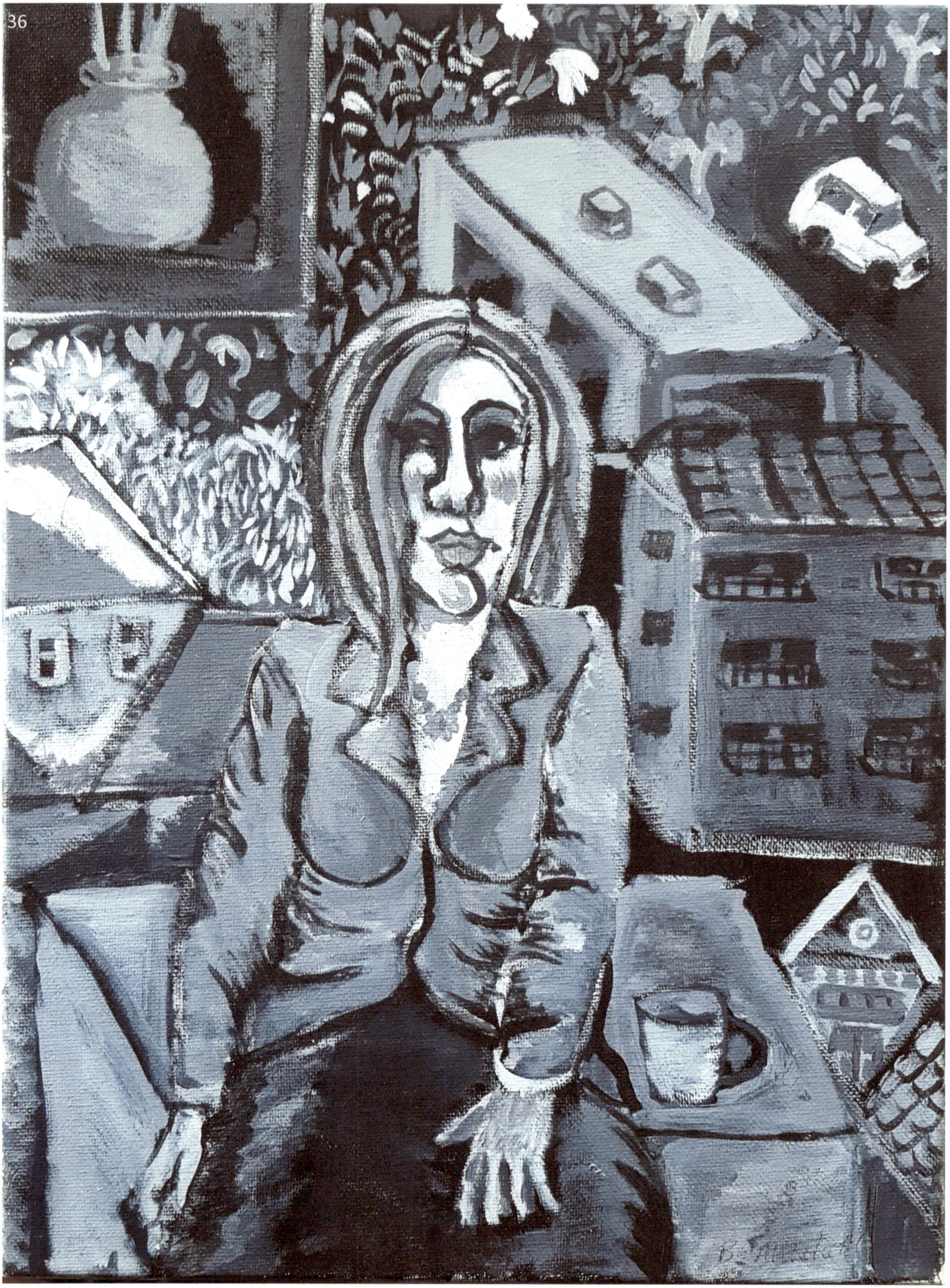

Mary, ca. 2019. Acrylic

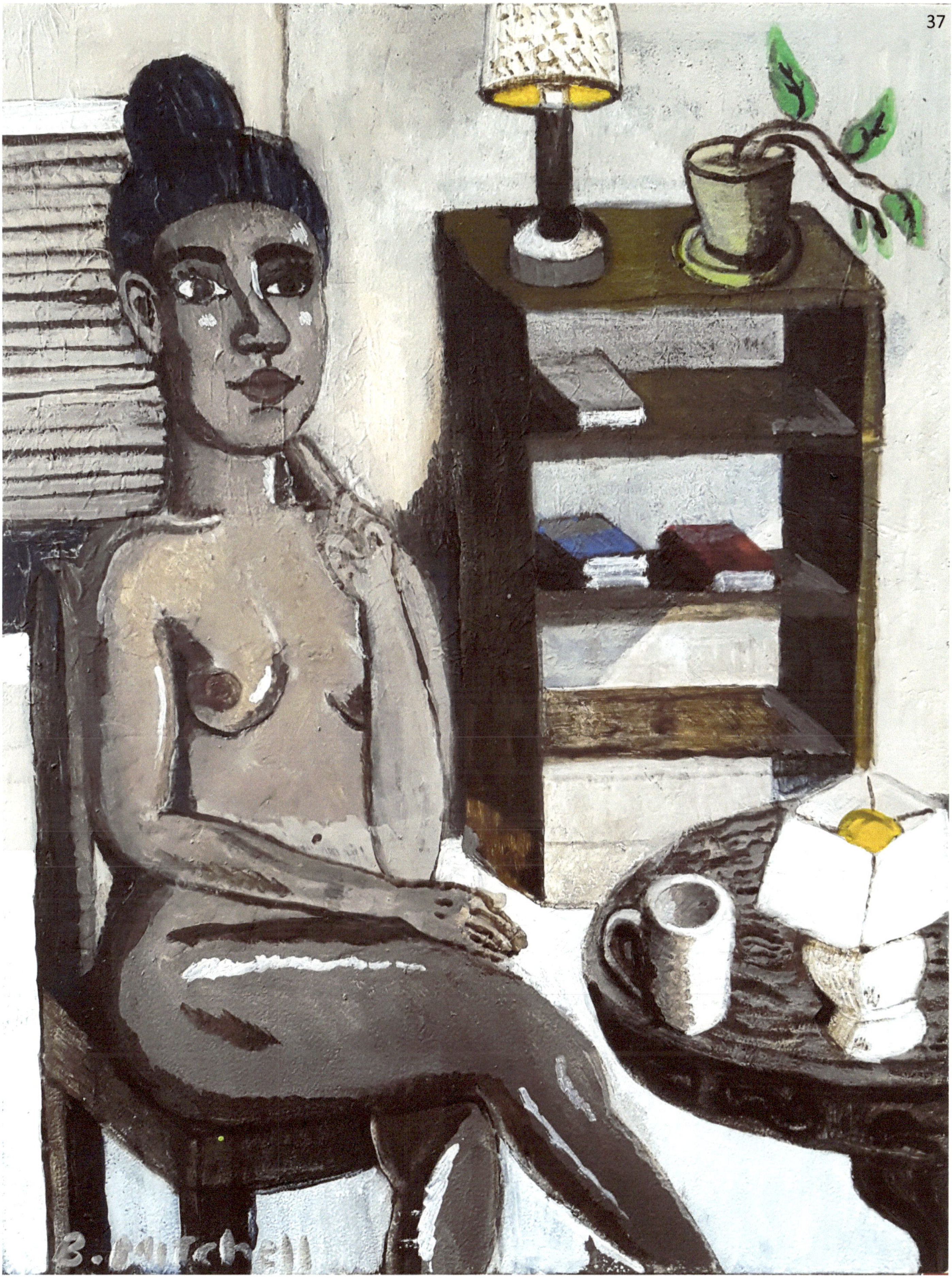

Title unknown, ca. 2019. Acrylic

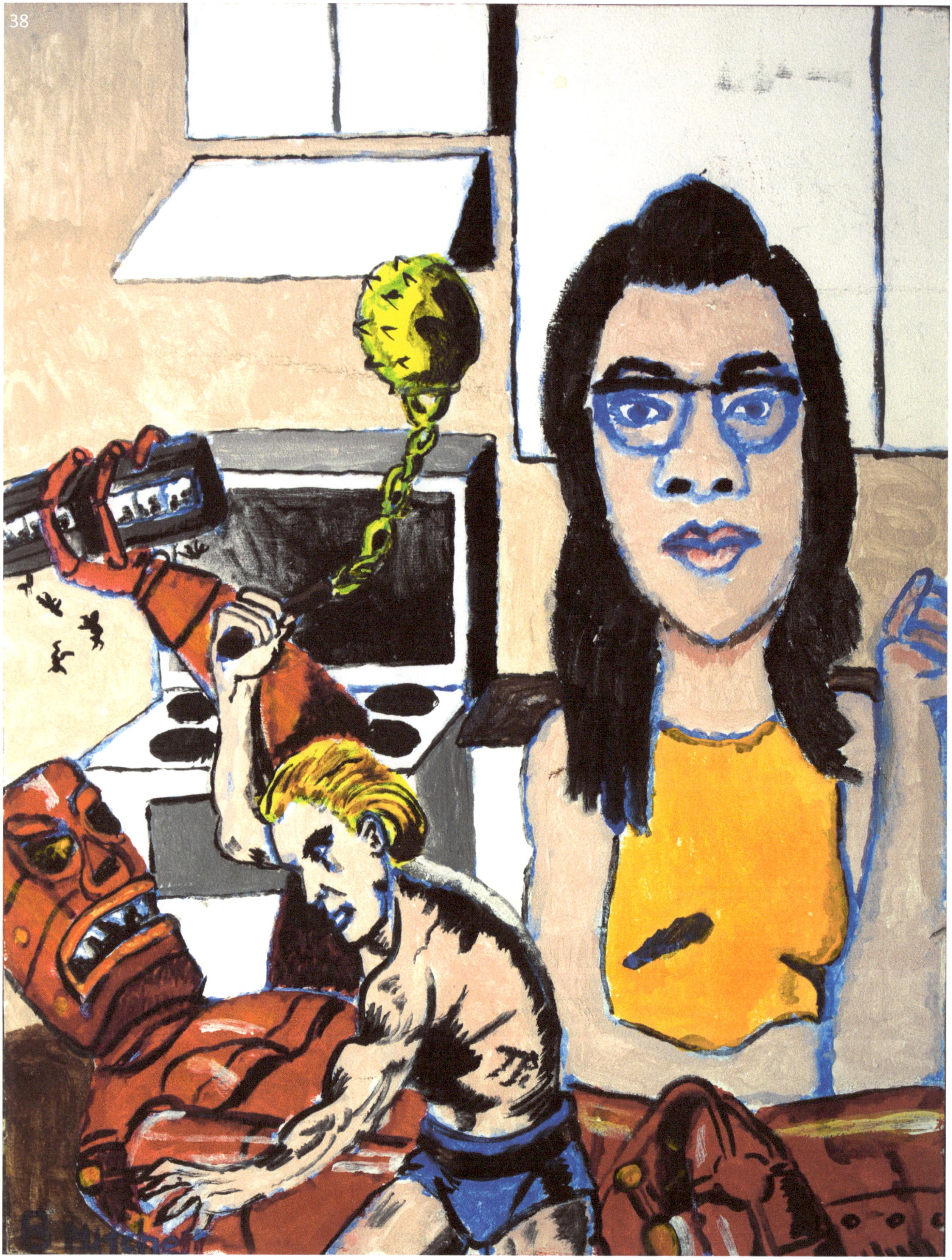

Invasion of Space Aliens, ca. 2019. Acrylic

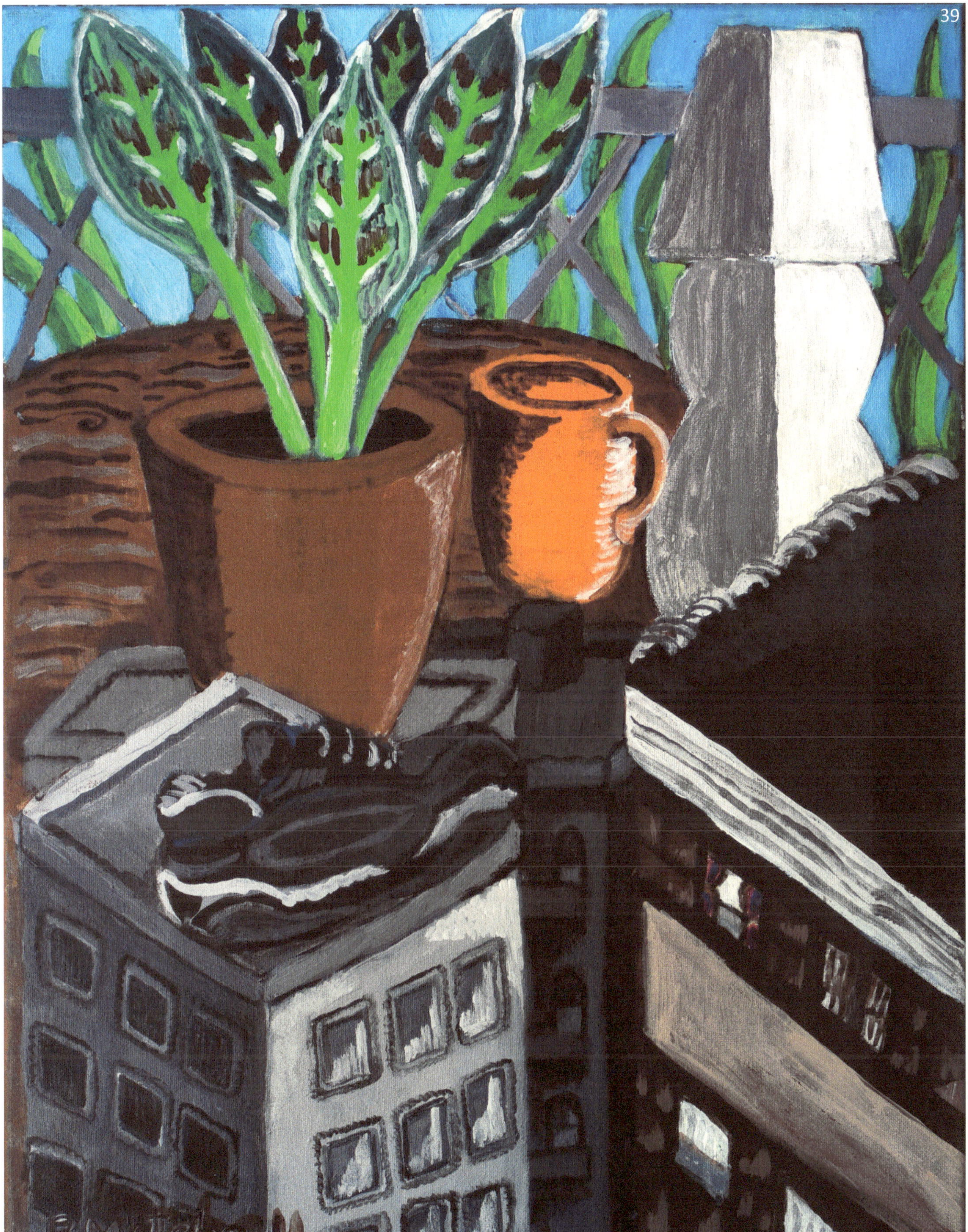

The View from My Kitchen Table, ca. 2019. Acrylic on canvas

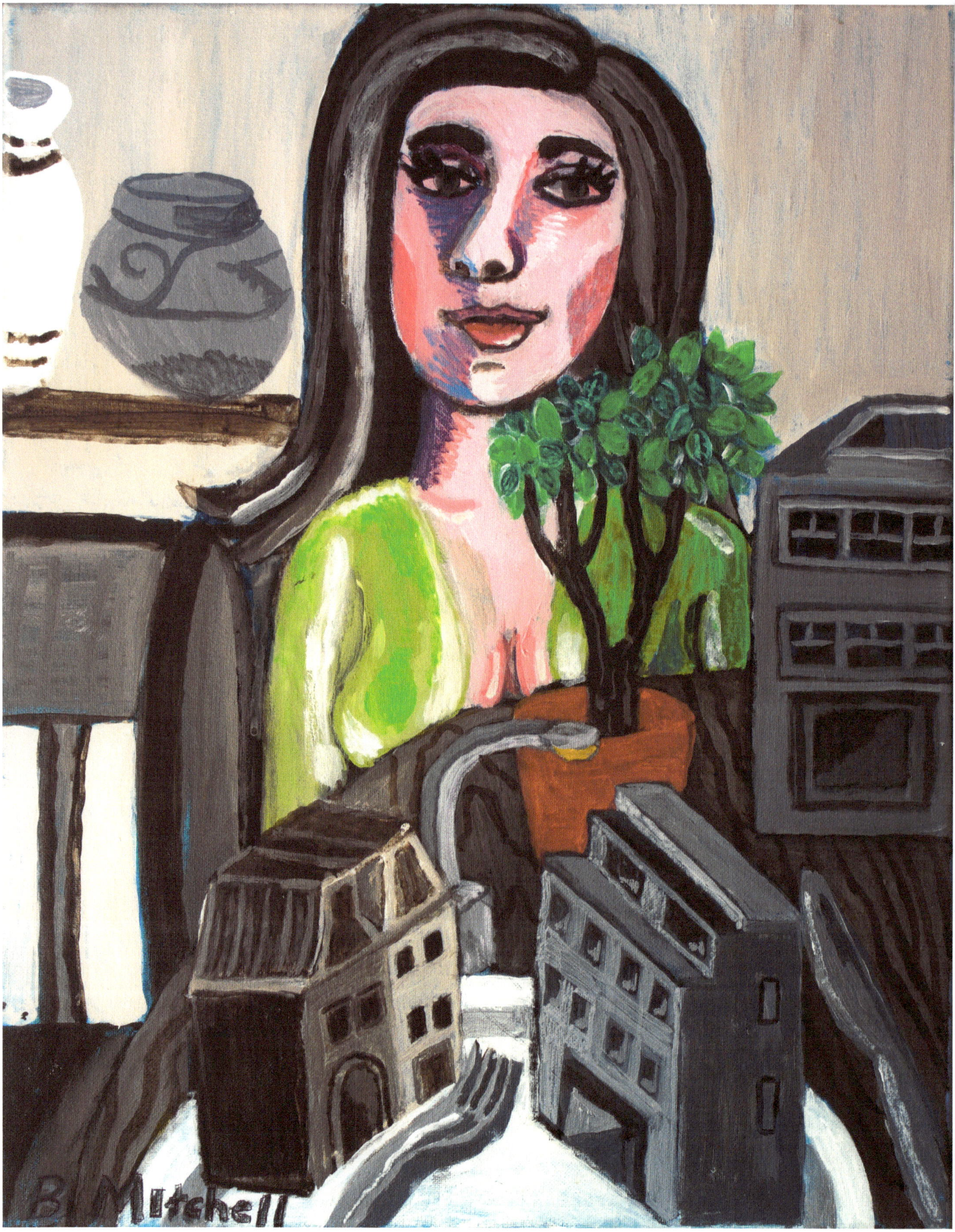

Peace, 2019. Acrylic

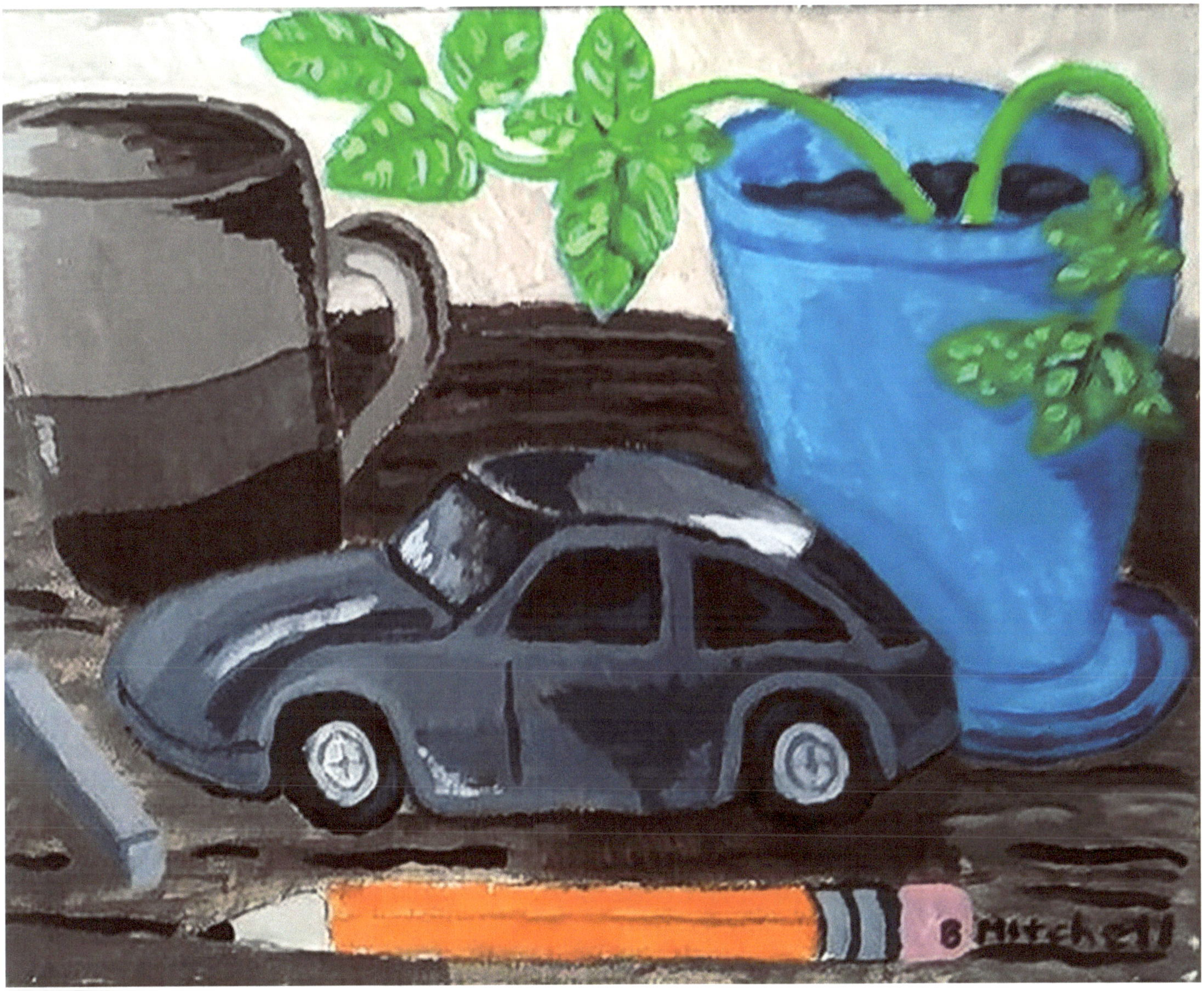

Title unknown, 2019. Acrylic

"A world within a world. Double parked in-between my coffee and my plant on my kitchen table"

B. Mitchell, 2019

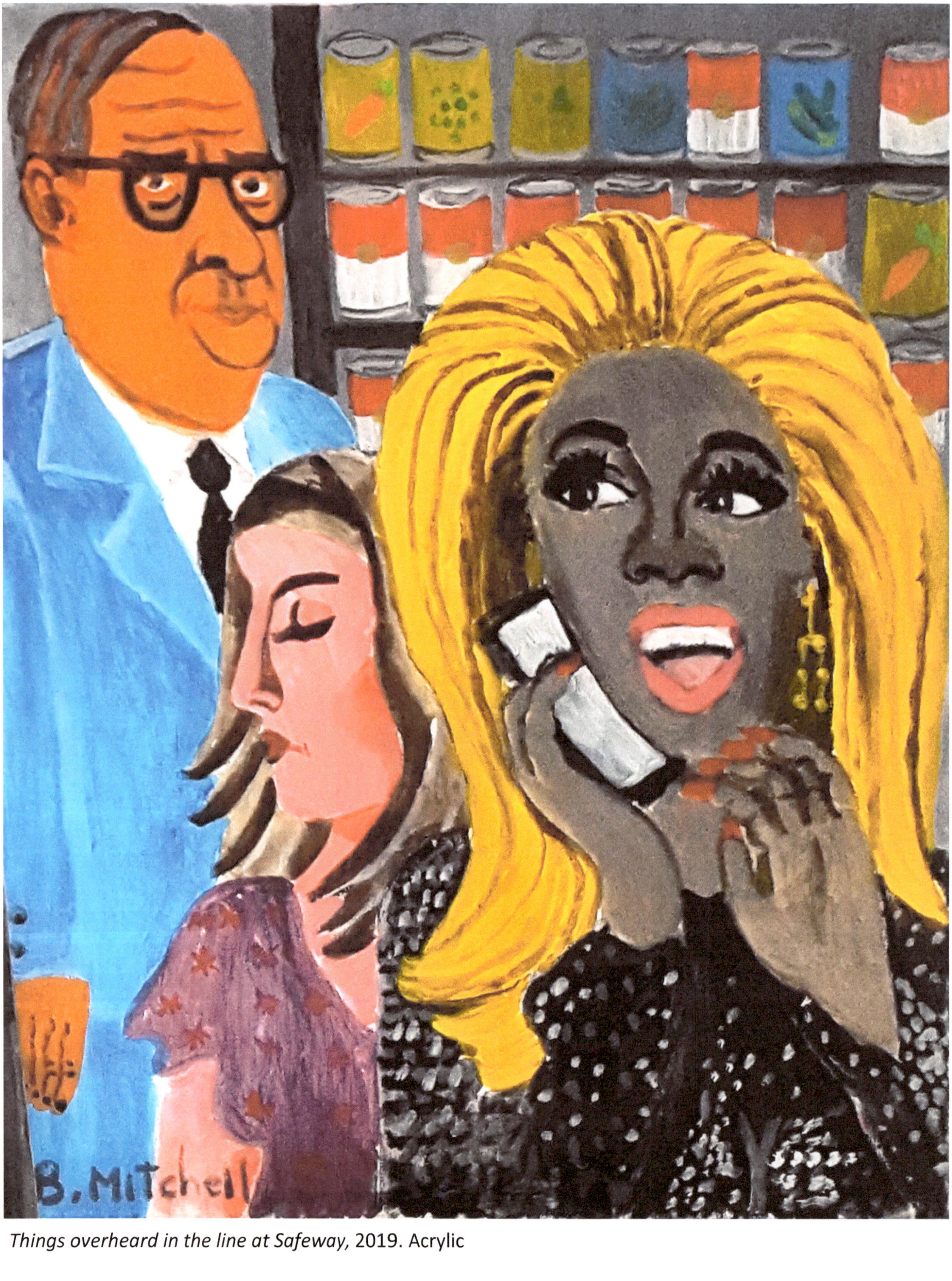

Things overheard in the line at Safeway, 2019. Acrylic

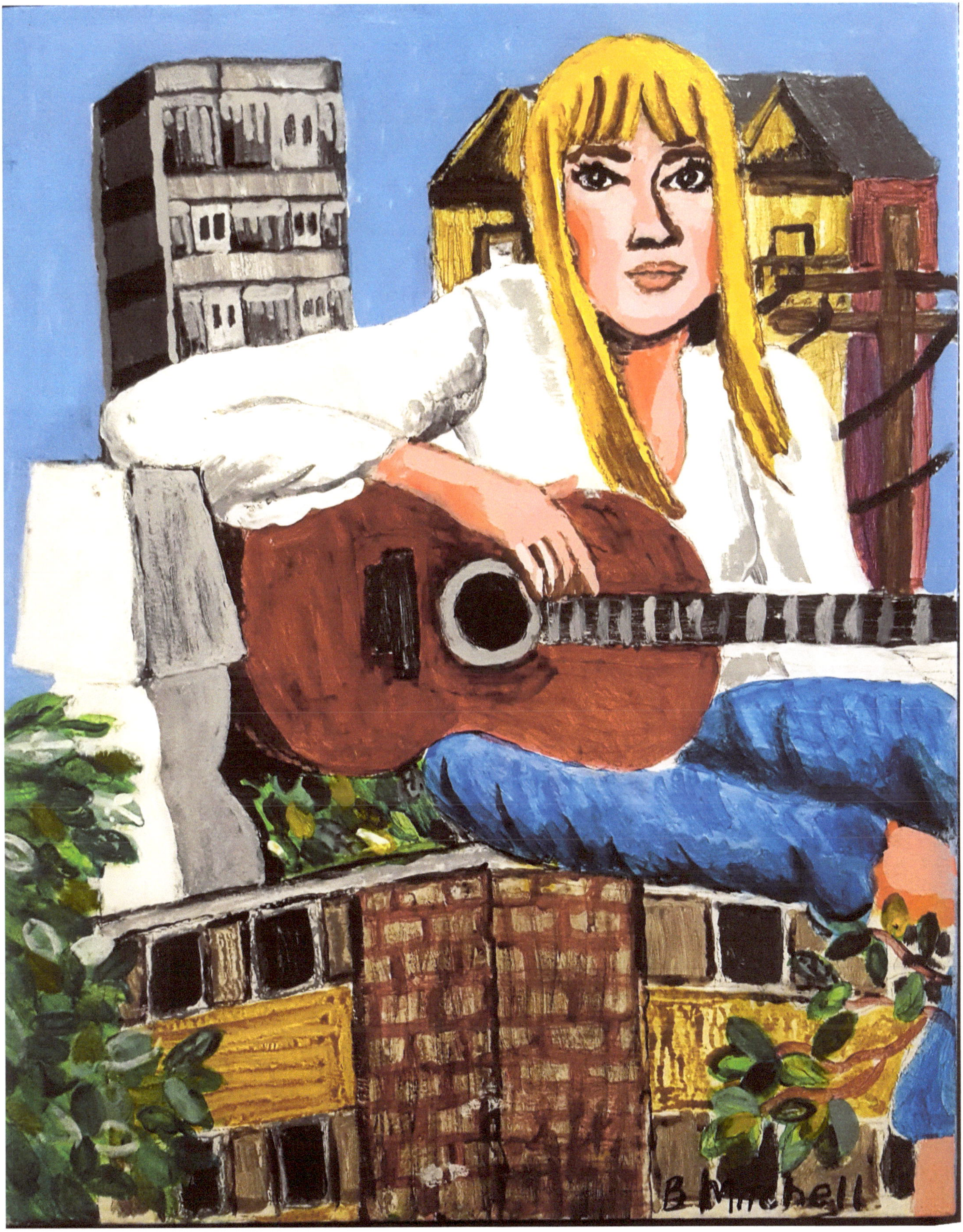

Jasper Avenue and 95 Street , 2019. Acrylic

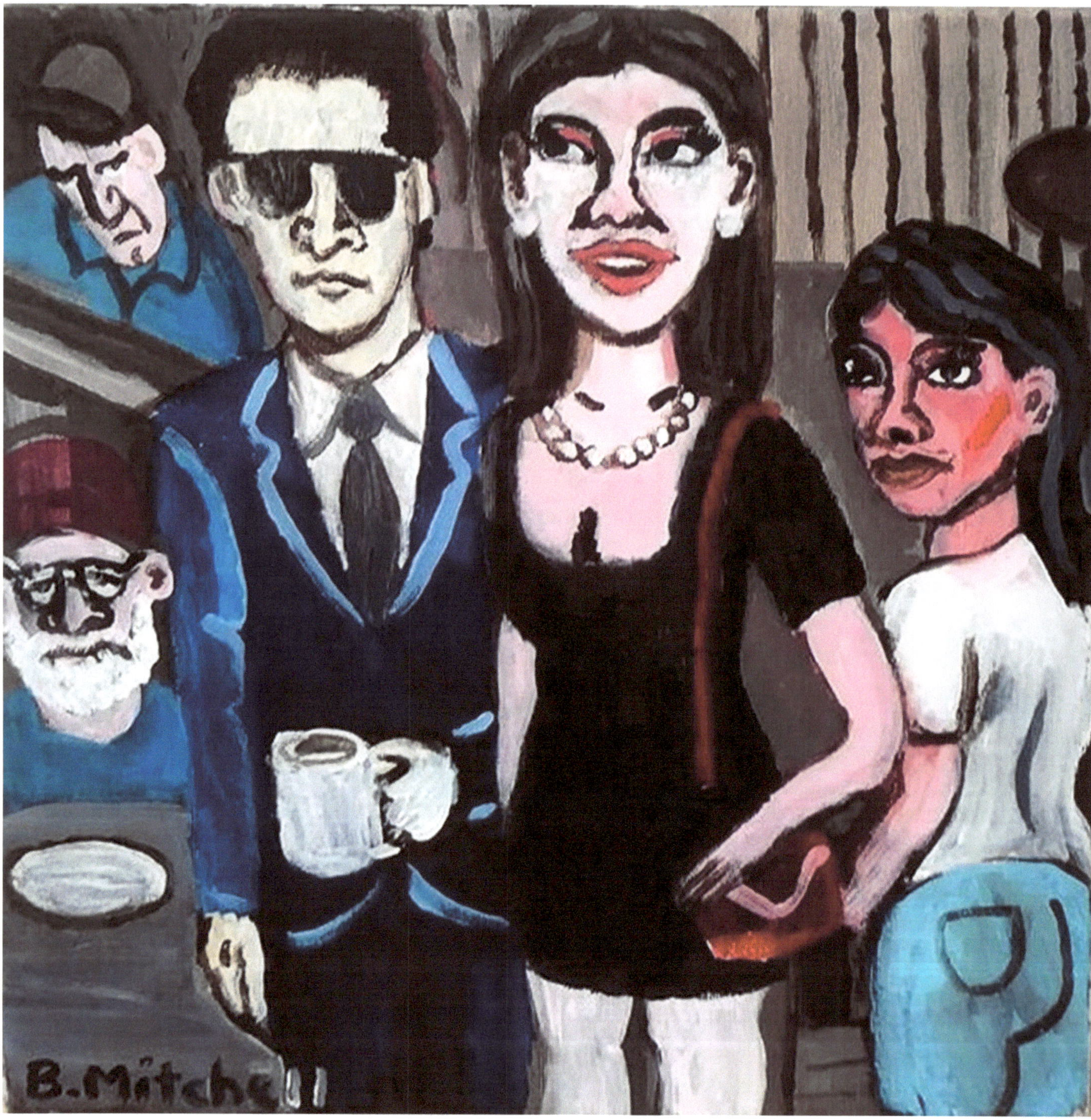

Dinner at The Mustard Seed, 2019. Acrylic

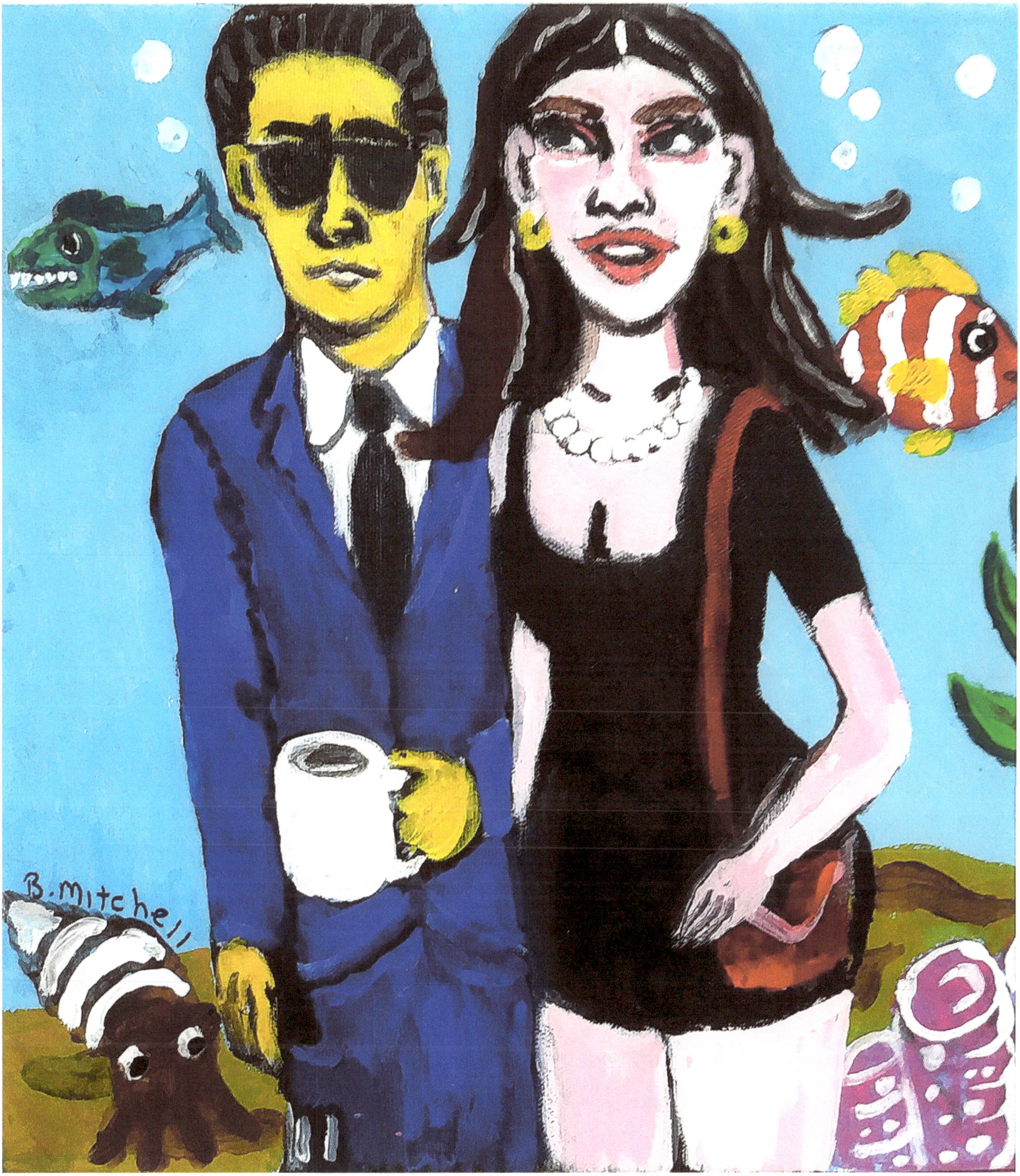

Under the Sea, 2019. Acrylic

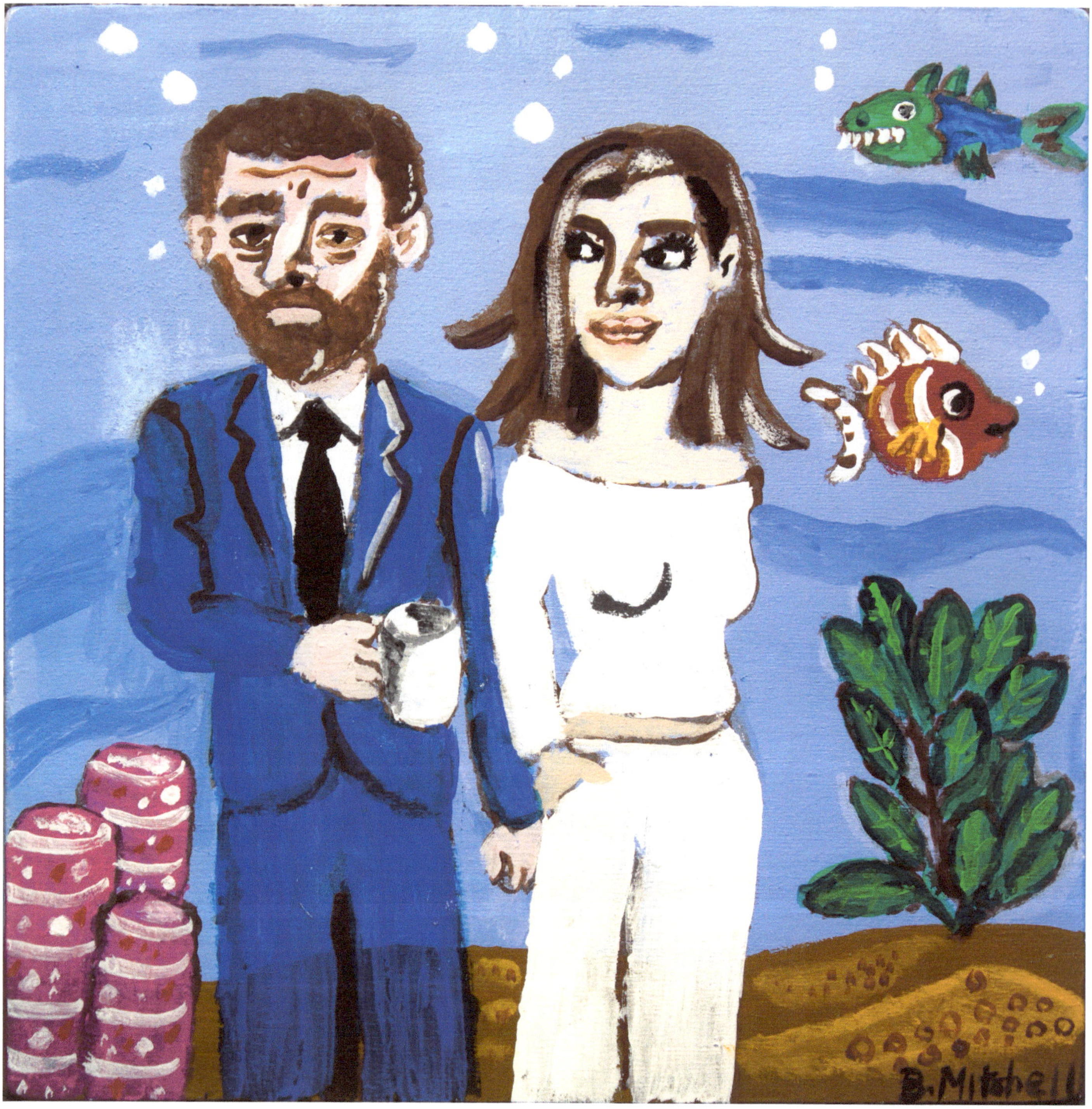

Under the Sea II, 2019. Acrylic

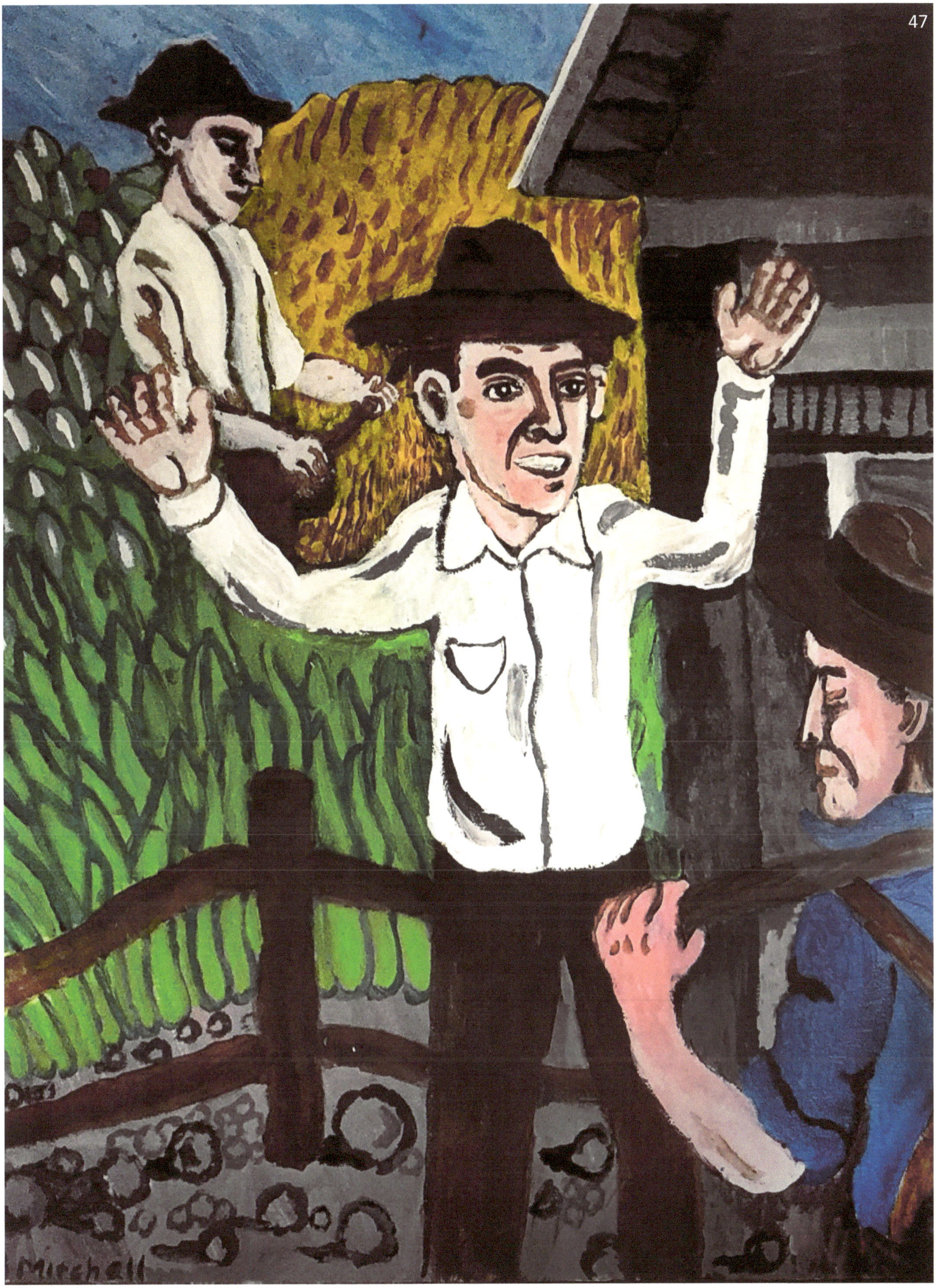

The Prodigal Son, 2019. Acrylic

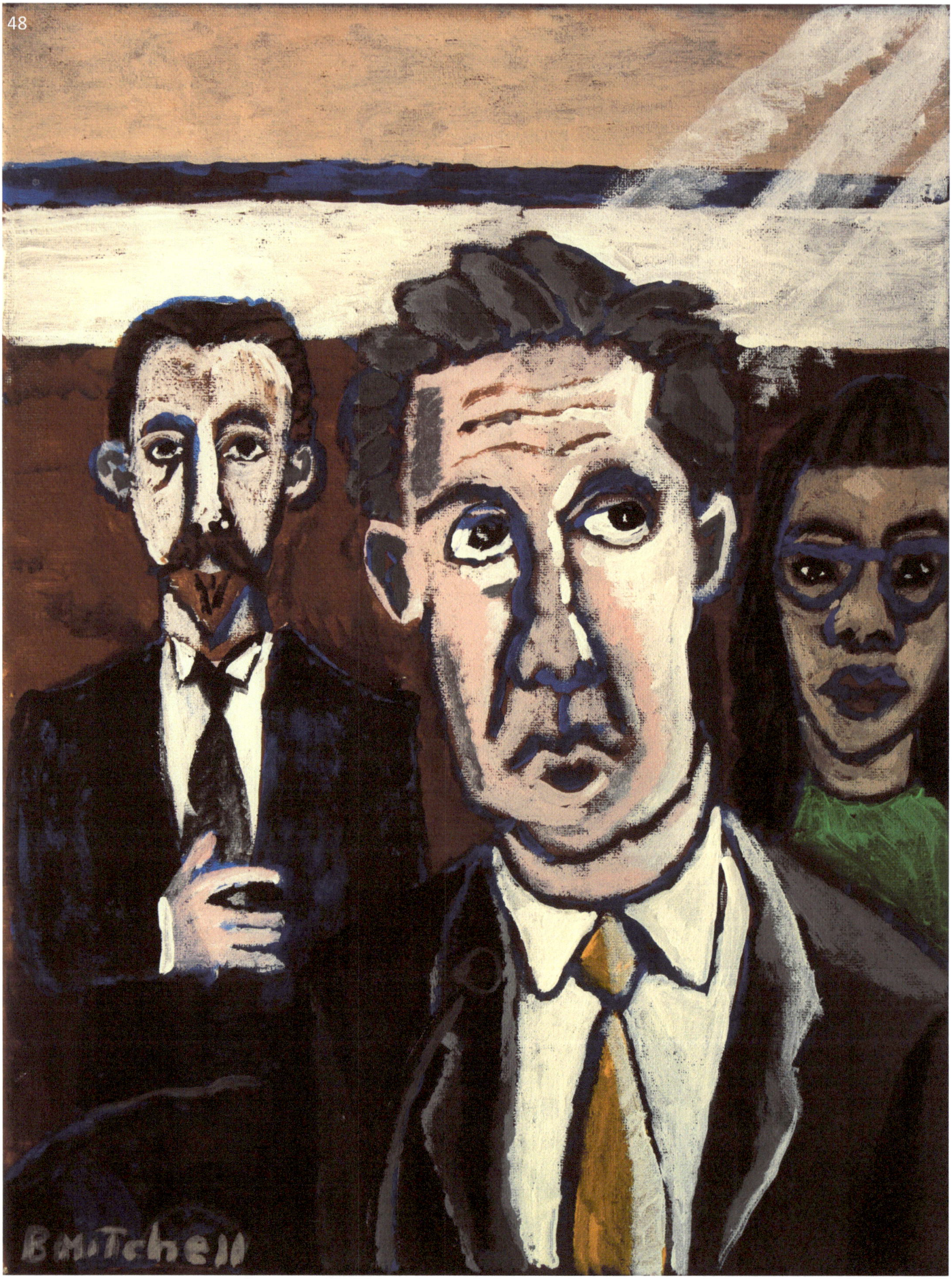

The Redemption of Michael Cohen, 2019. Acrylic on canvas

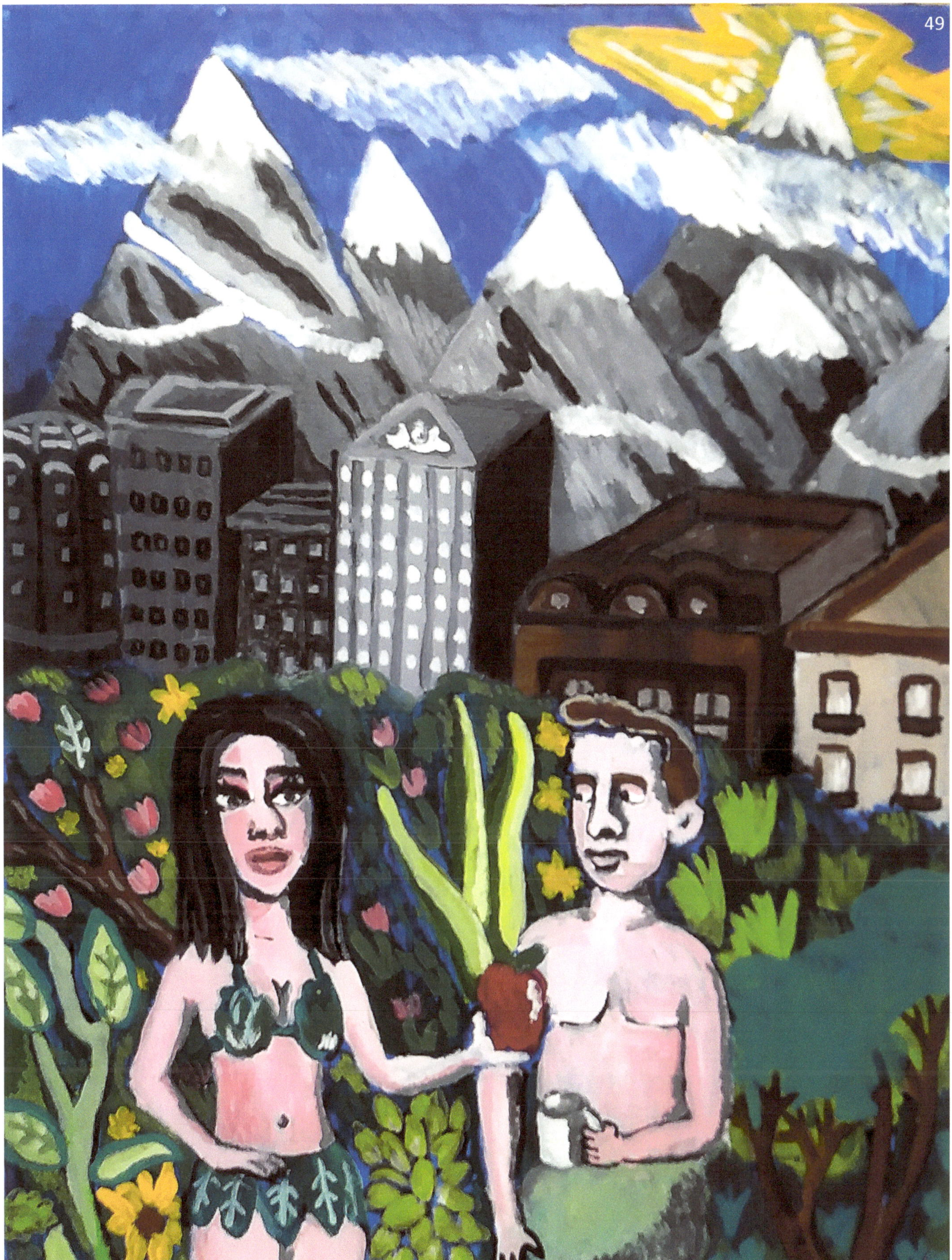

Modern Adam and Eve, 2019. Acrylic

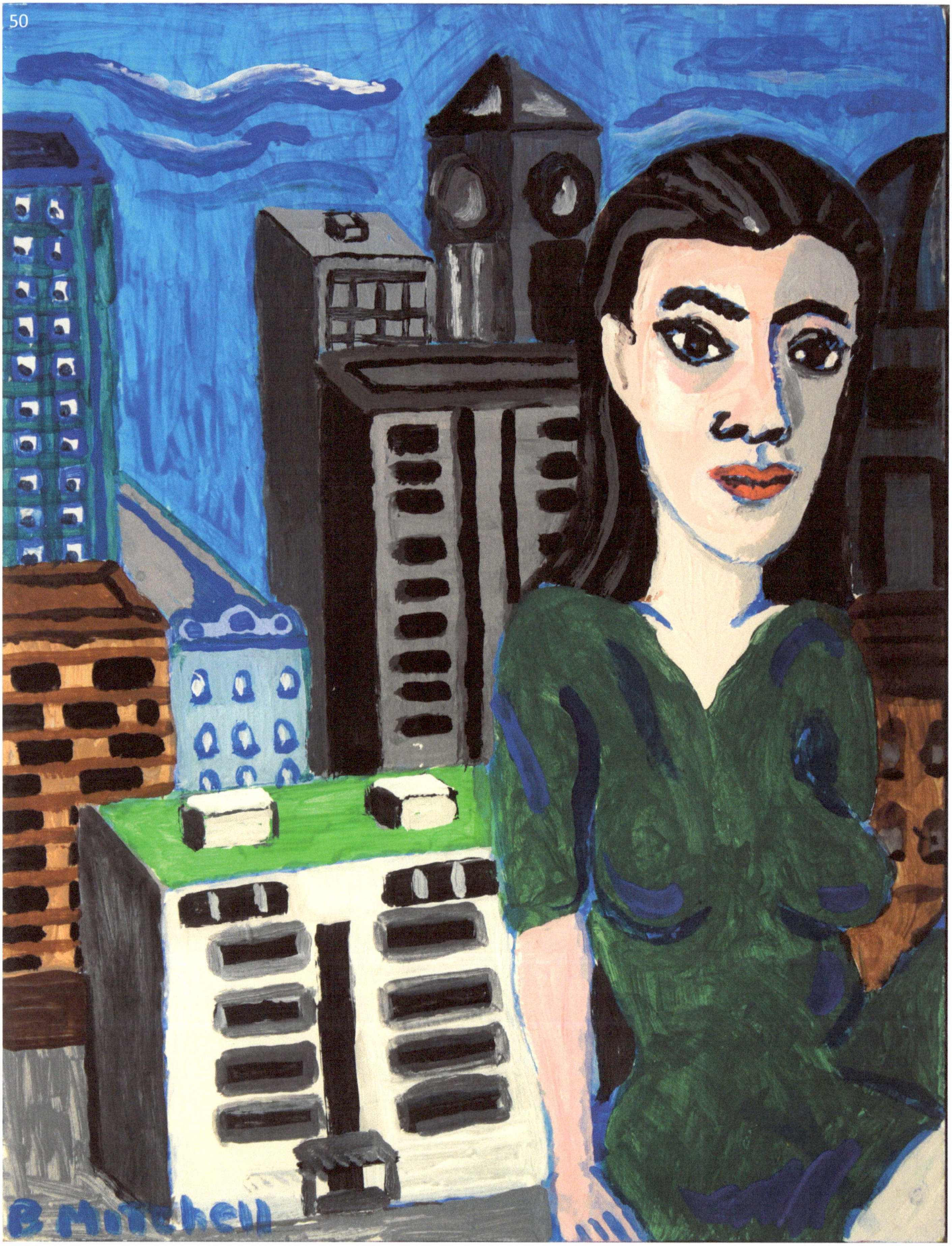

At Ease in Edmonton. 2019. Acrylic

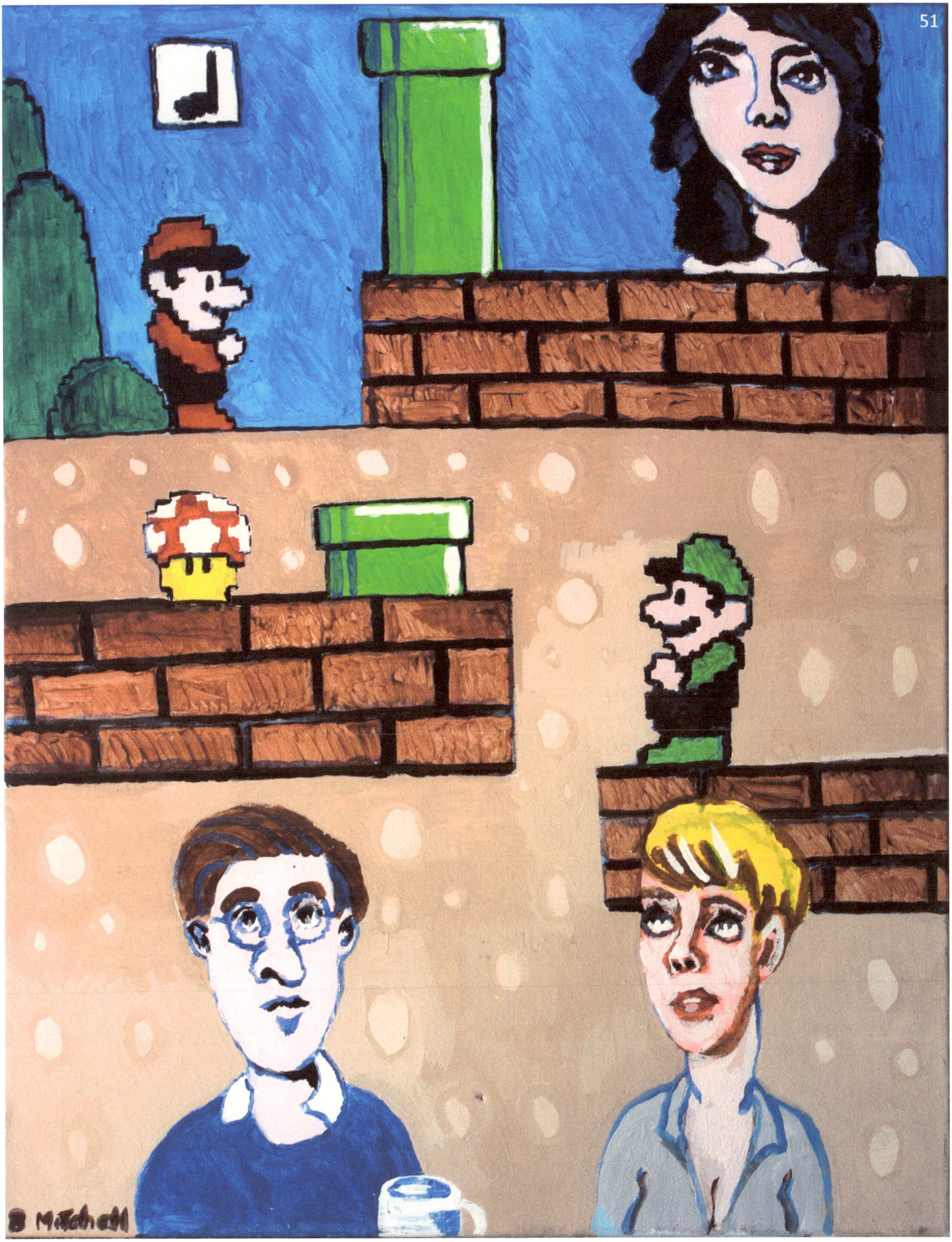

Disposable Culture, ca. 2019, Acrylic on canvas

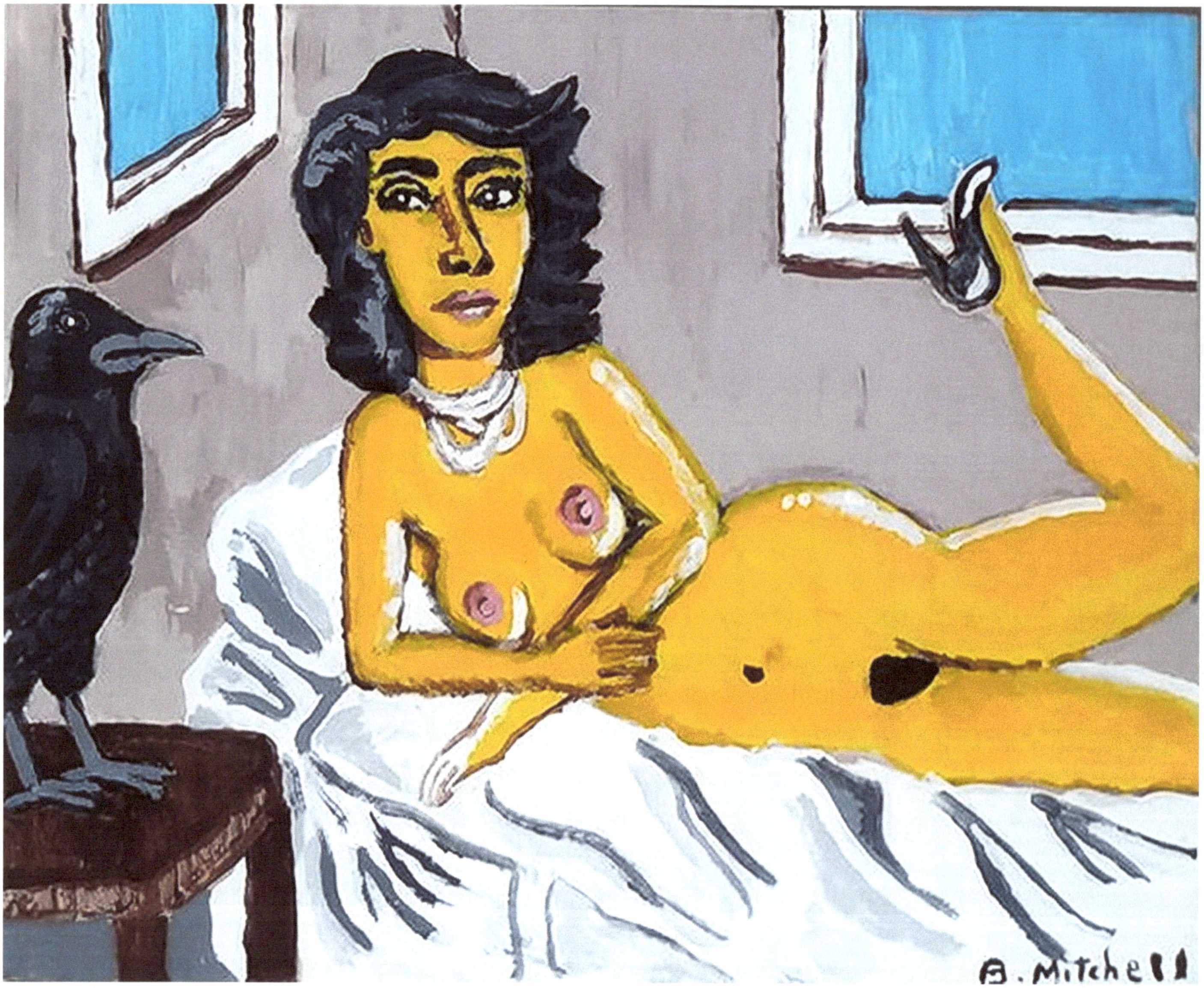

Title unknown. 2019. Acrylic

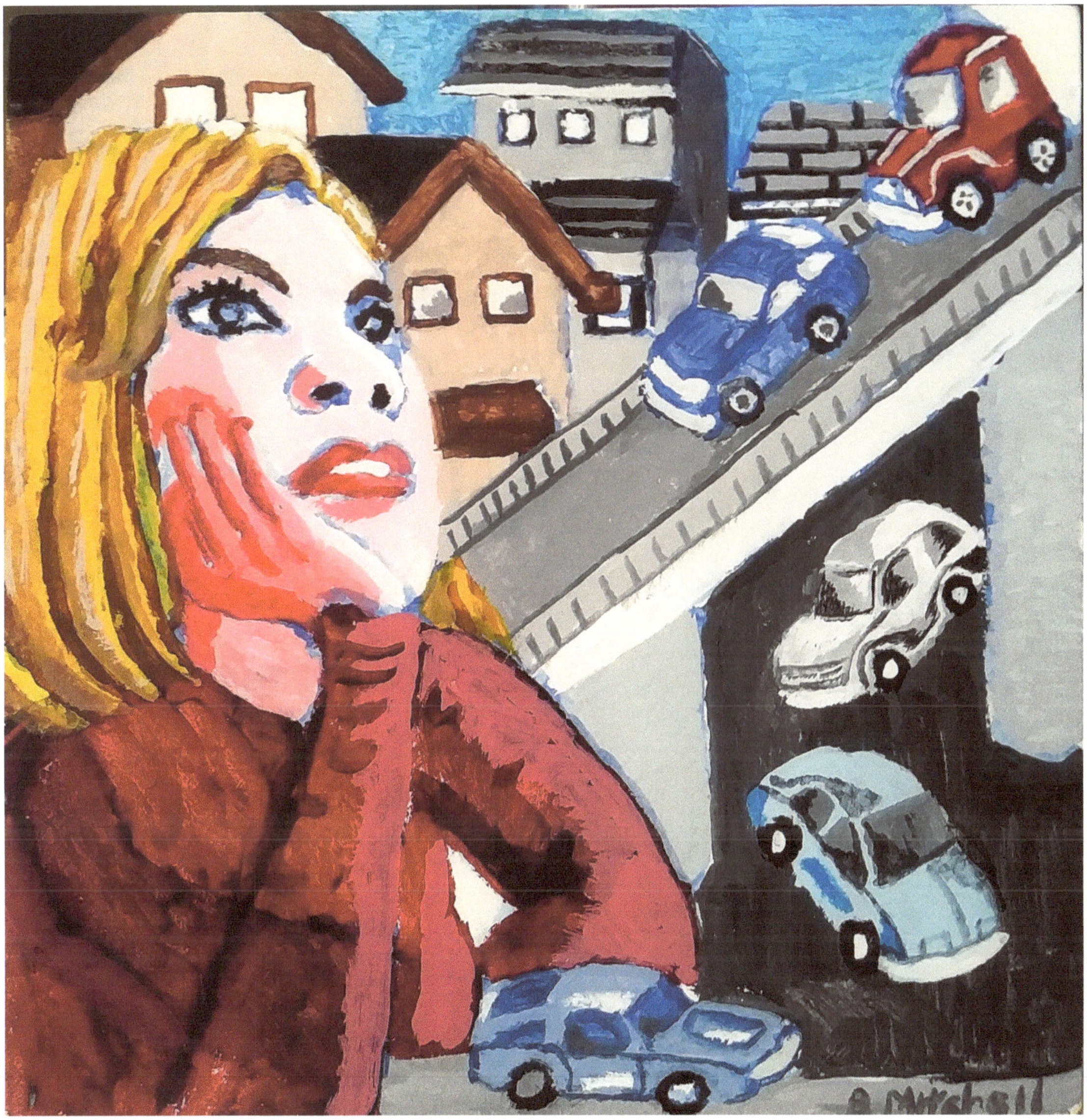

Daydreaming, 2019. Acrylic

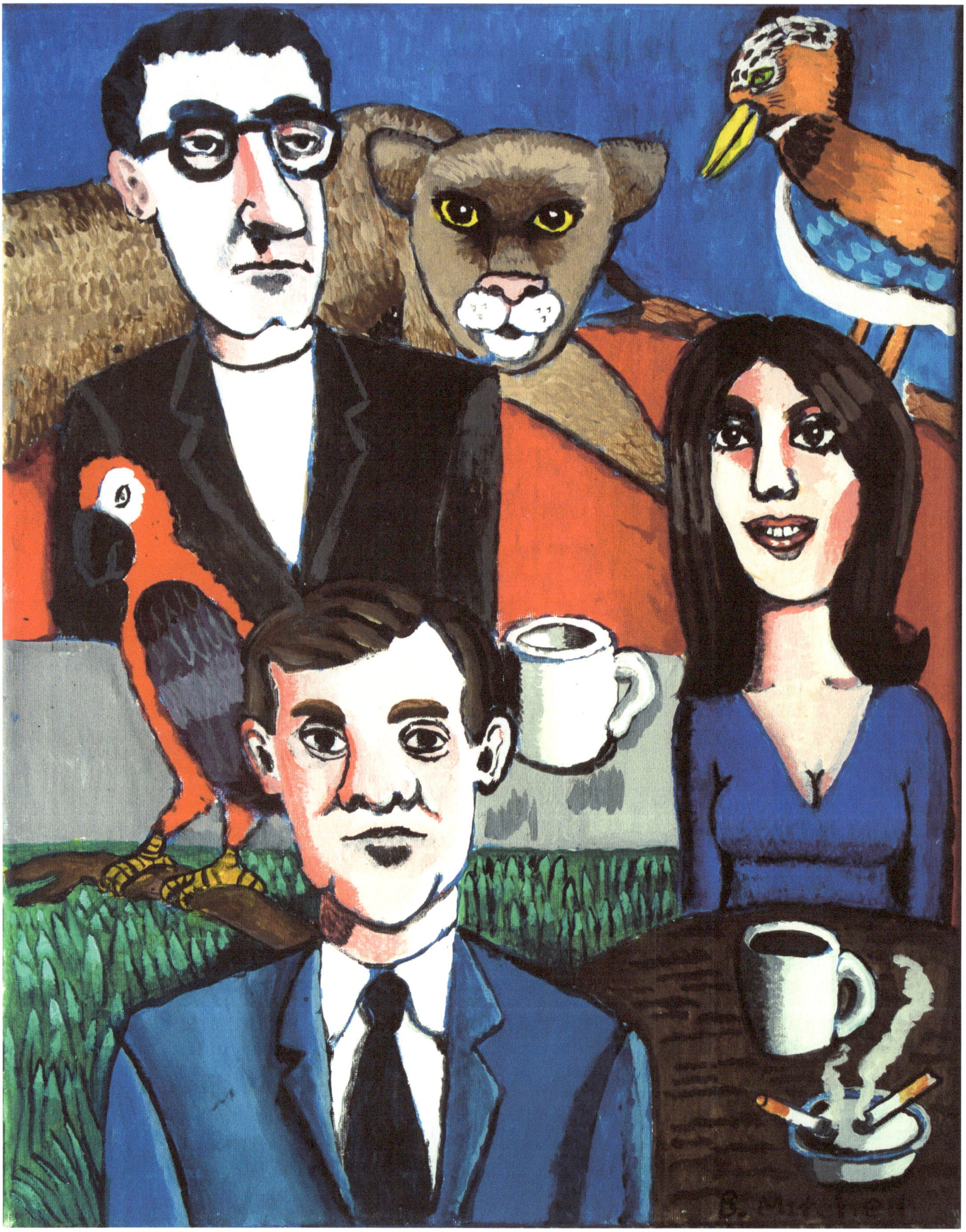

Call of the Wild. 2019. Acrylic

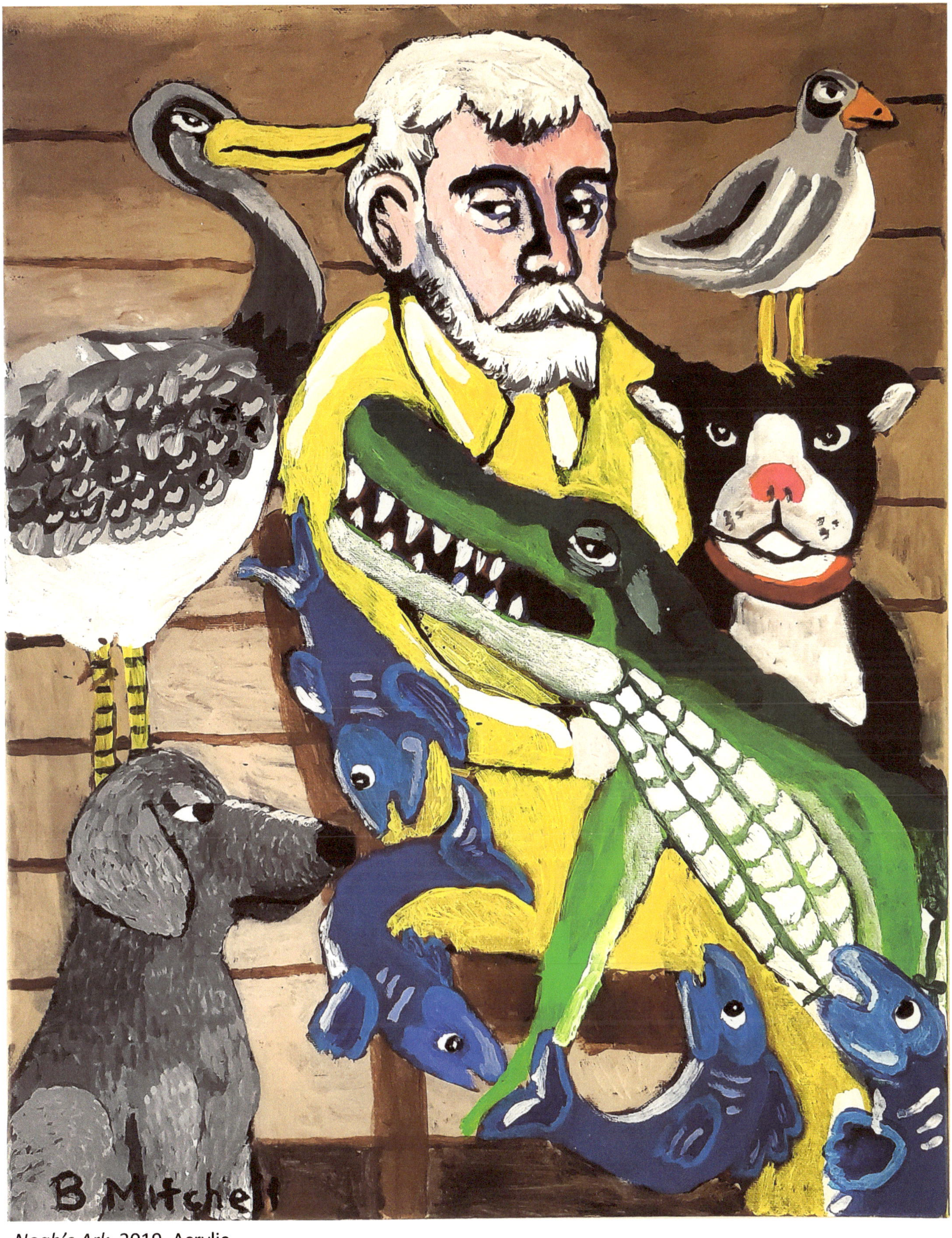

Noah's Ark, 2019. Acrylic

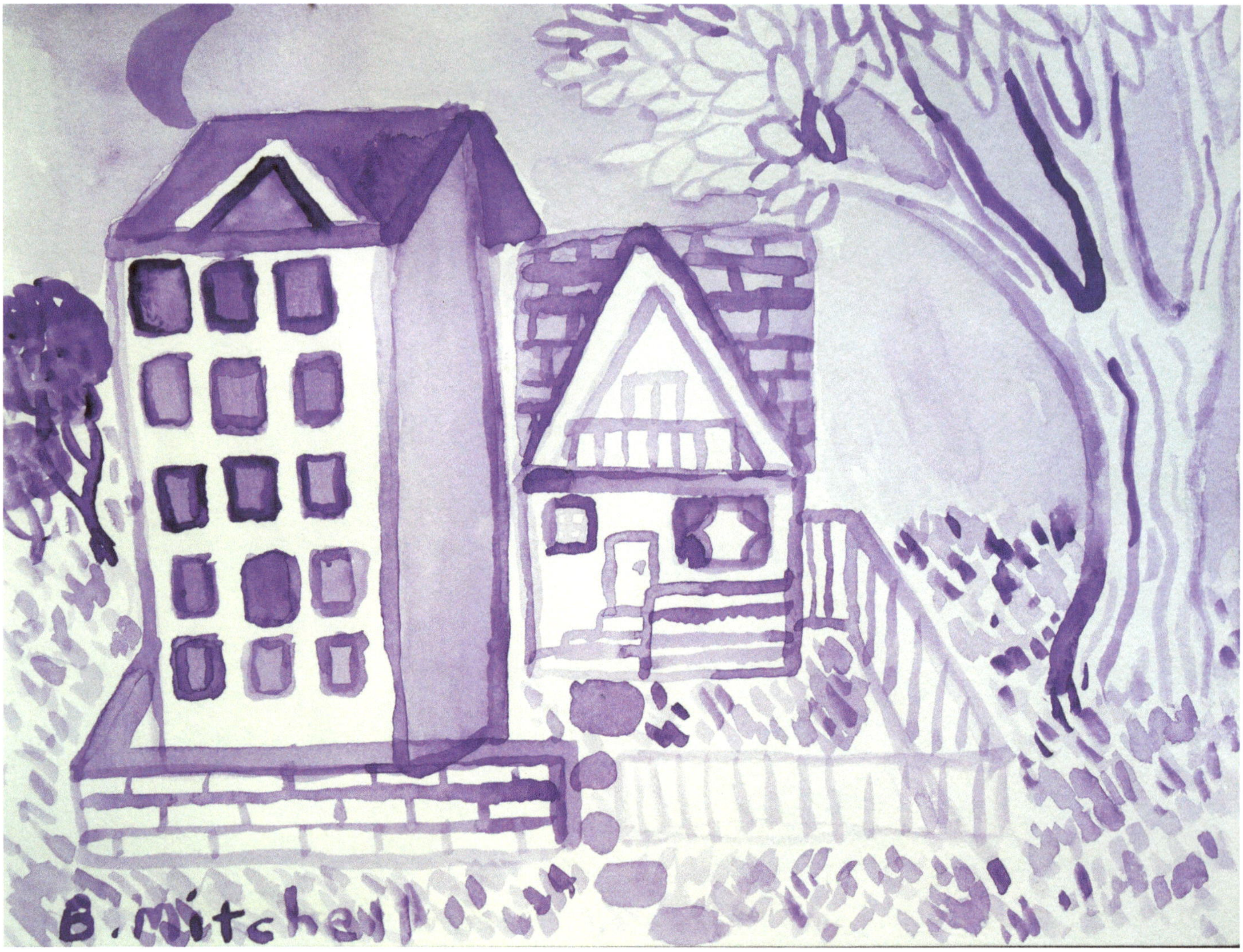

Untitled, ca. 2020. Watercolour

"...at one of the art nights, it was quiet at the church and only me, Bruce and another artist Charles, were at the art table. Charles always struggles with what to do at art night and so that night, I suggested to Bruce that he give Charles and I an art lesson. Bruce immediately liked the idea and started us off with choosing our paint color and then watering it down to the right paint/water ratio. He then began to instruct each step he was painting, encouraging us as we went along. The end result was that both Charles and I were given an amazing art lesson that night by Bruce. I encouraged Bruce to consider teaching art as he contemplated what he wanted to do in the future as he had demonstrated a gift of teaching that night.

I still have my copy of the artwork from that night. It has a very special meaning to me of art night with Bruce. "

R. de Leon, Mustard Seed Art Group Volunteer Coordinator .

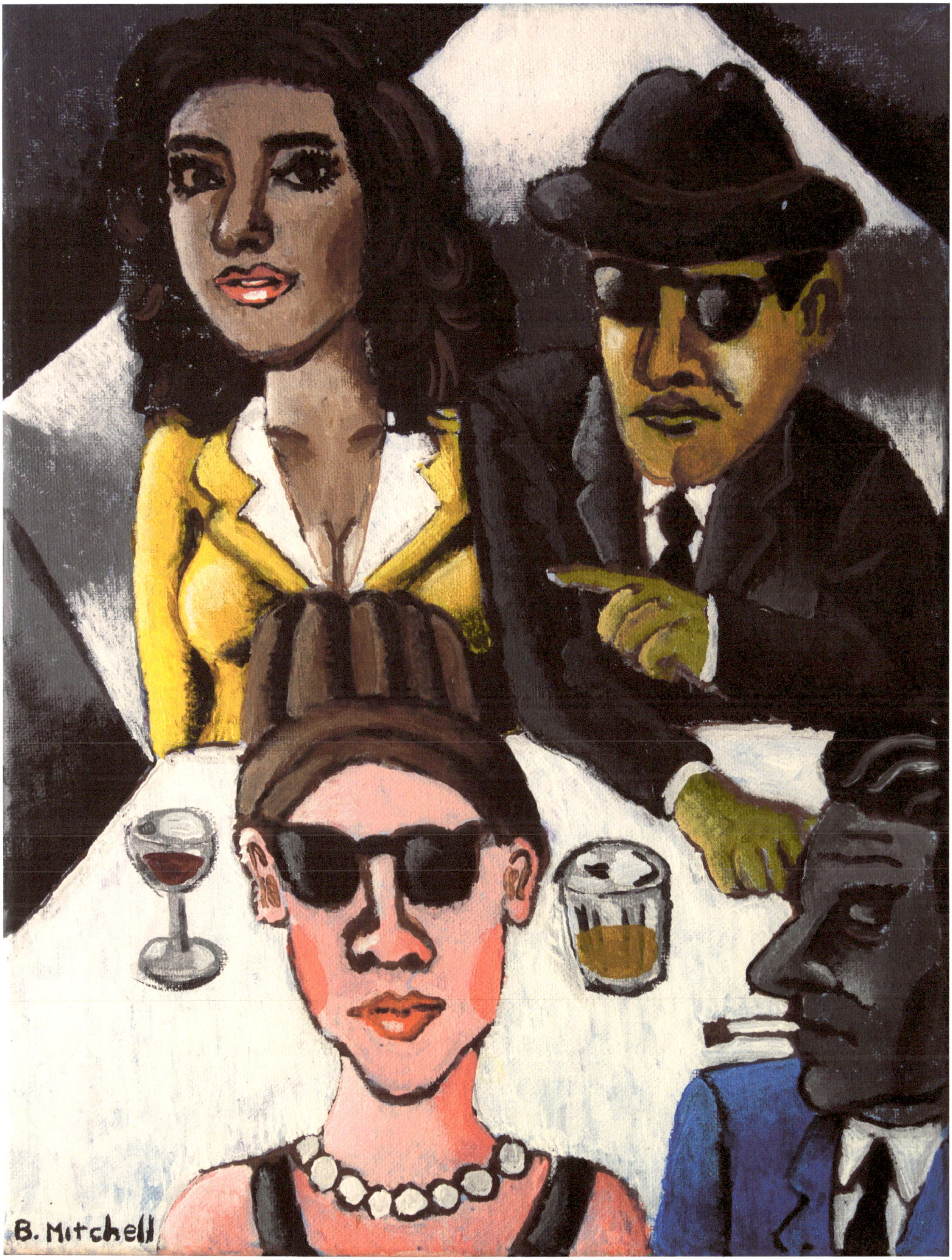

The Mobsters, 2020. Acrylic

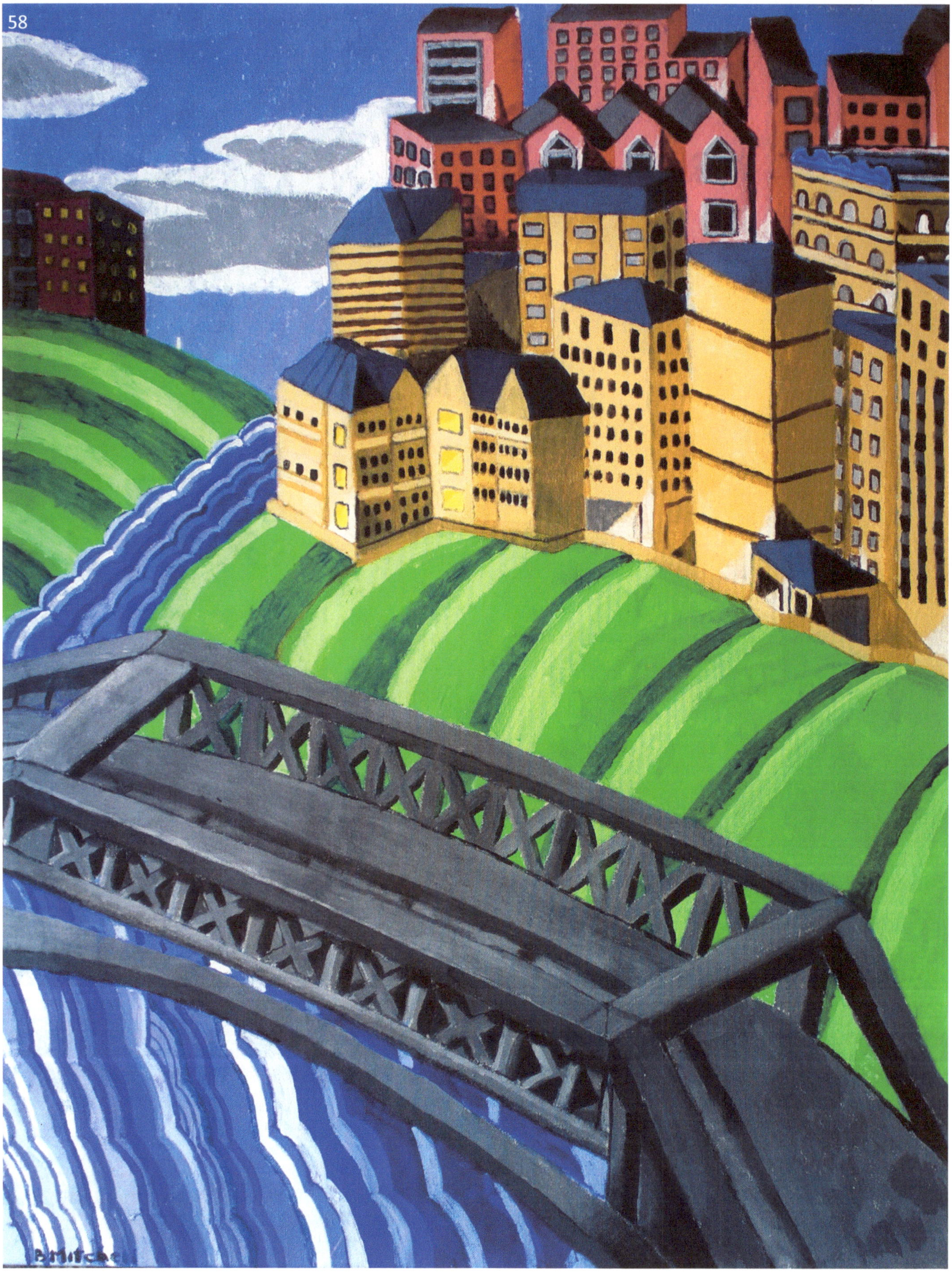

Untitled, 2020. Acrylic on canvas
The city of Edmonton, looking up from the river valley

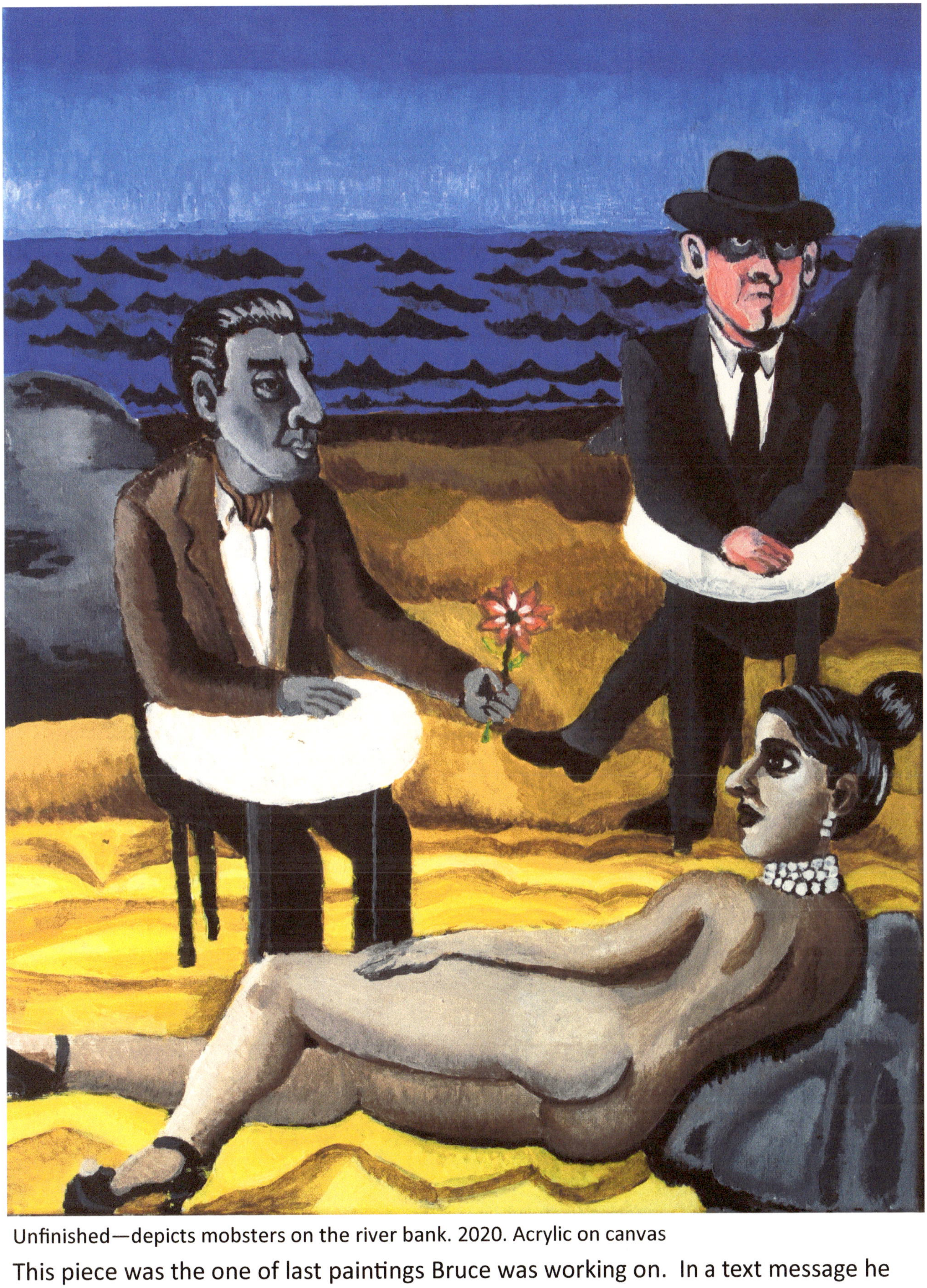

Unfinished—depicts mobsters on the river bank. 2020. Acrylic on canvas

This piece was the one of last paintings Bruce was working on. In a text message he describes it as "… my Jungian pychanalic [psychoanalytic] dream interpretation painting" B. Mitchell April, 2020.

Bruce's Sketch Book

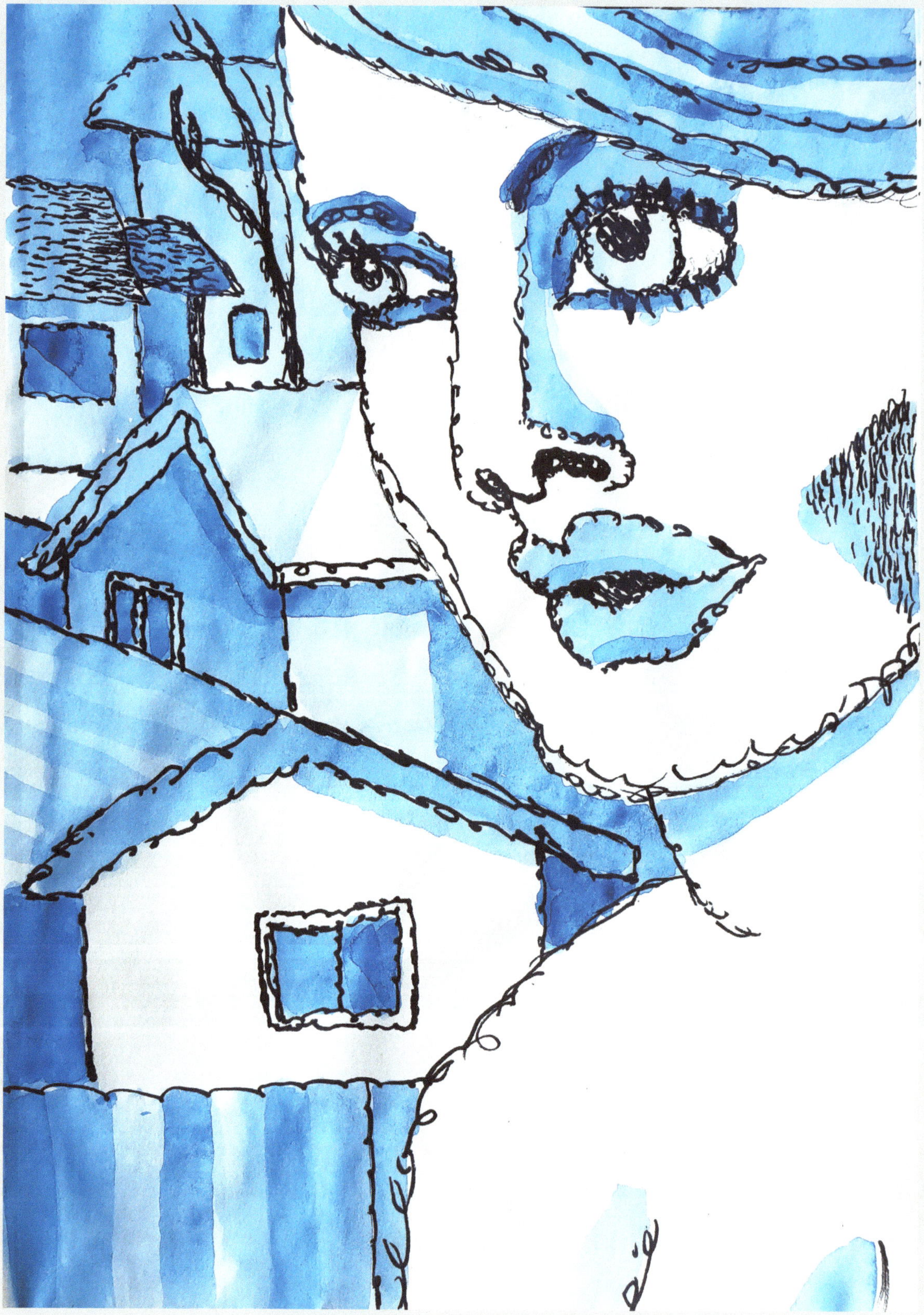

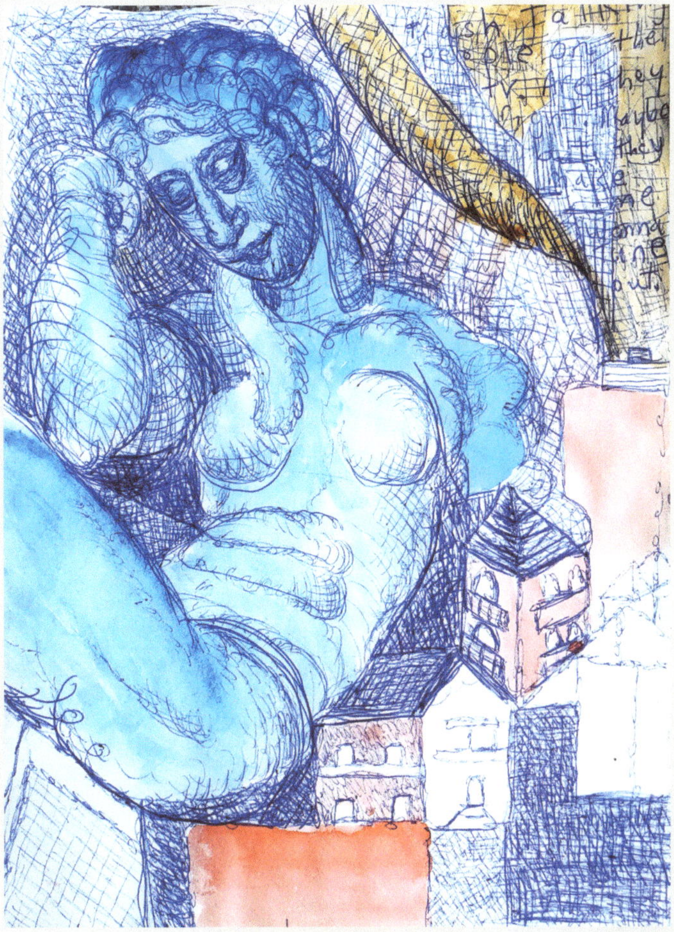

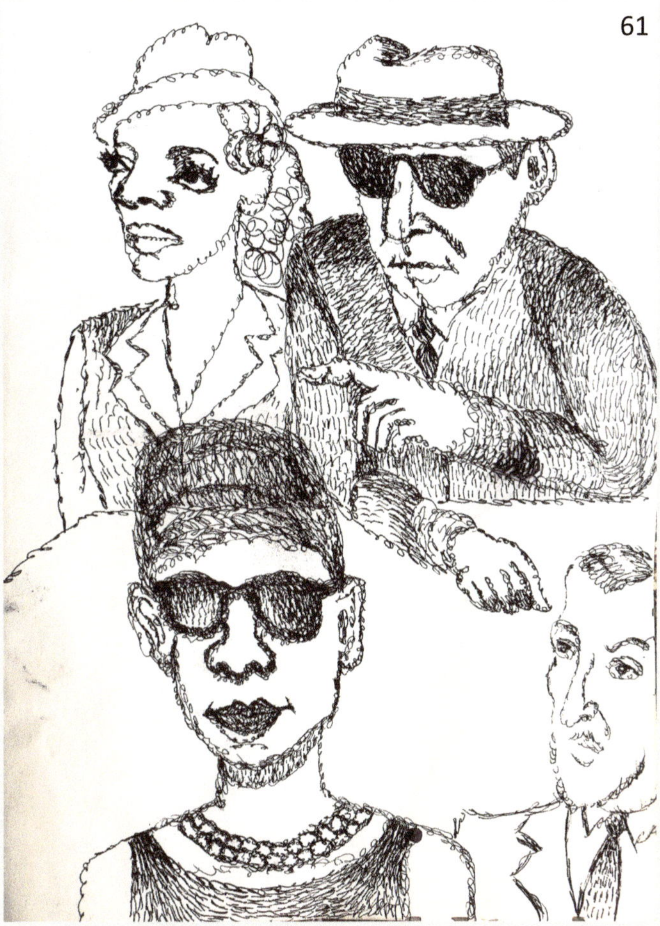

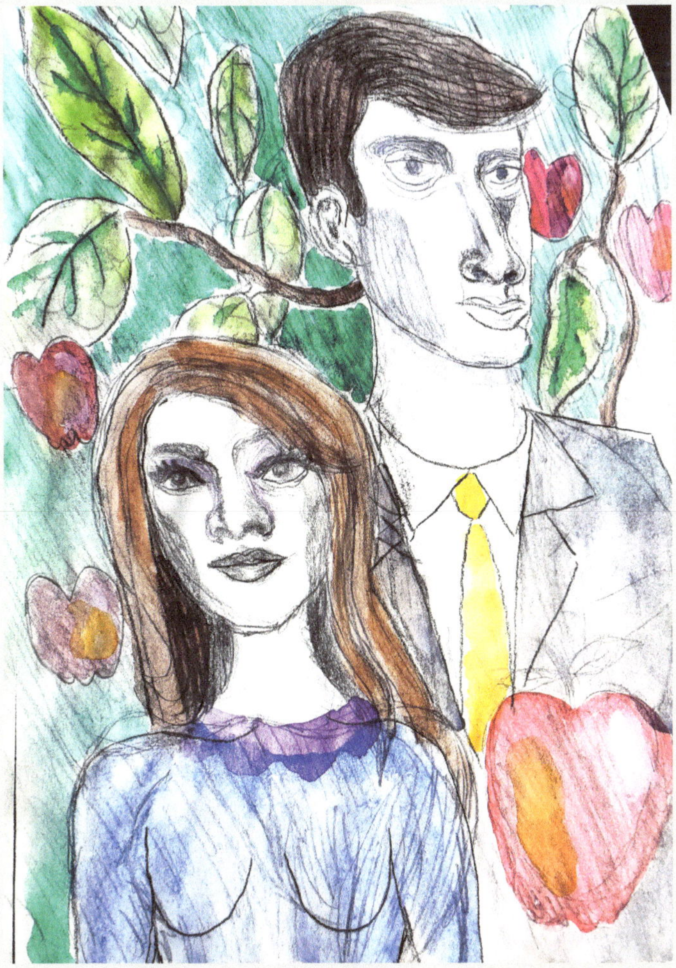

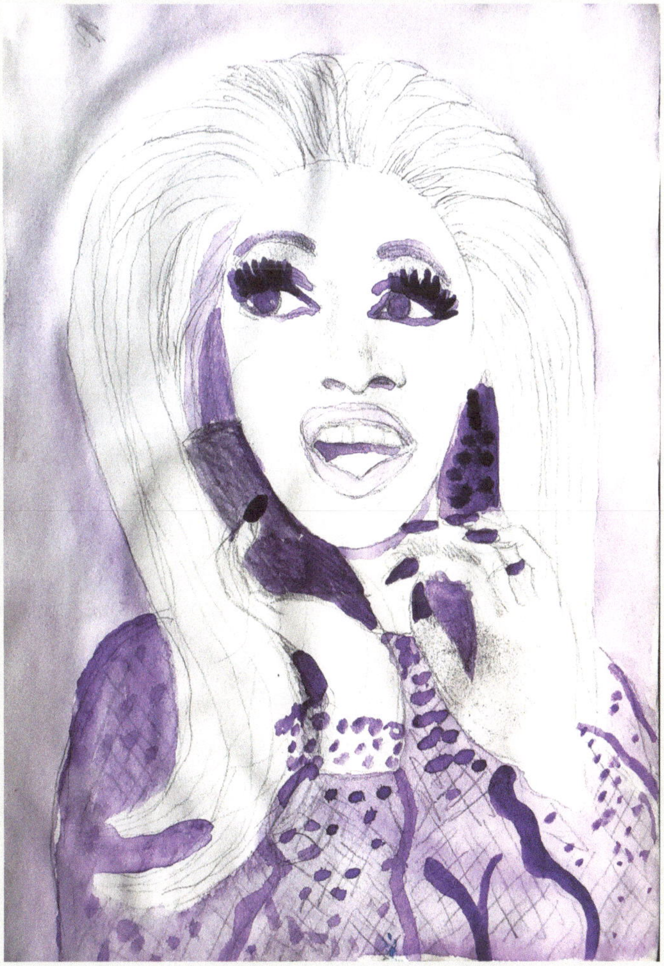

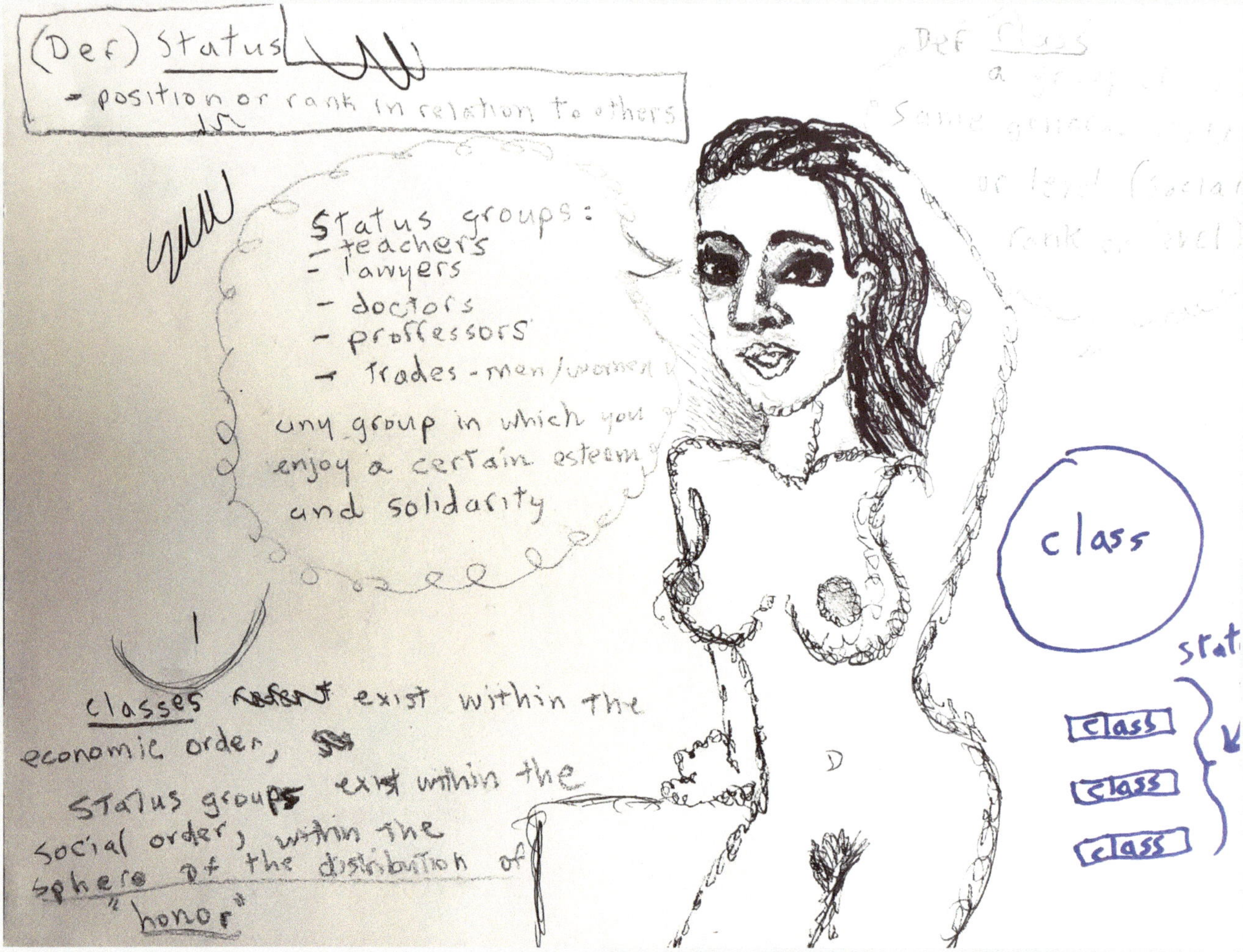
(Def) Status
- position or rank in relation to others
Status groups:
- teachers
- lawyers
- doctors
- proffessors
- trades-men/women
any group in which you enjoy a certain esteem and solidarity
classes exist within the economic order,
status groups exist within the social order, within the sphere of the distribution of "honor"
class
class
class
class

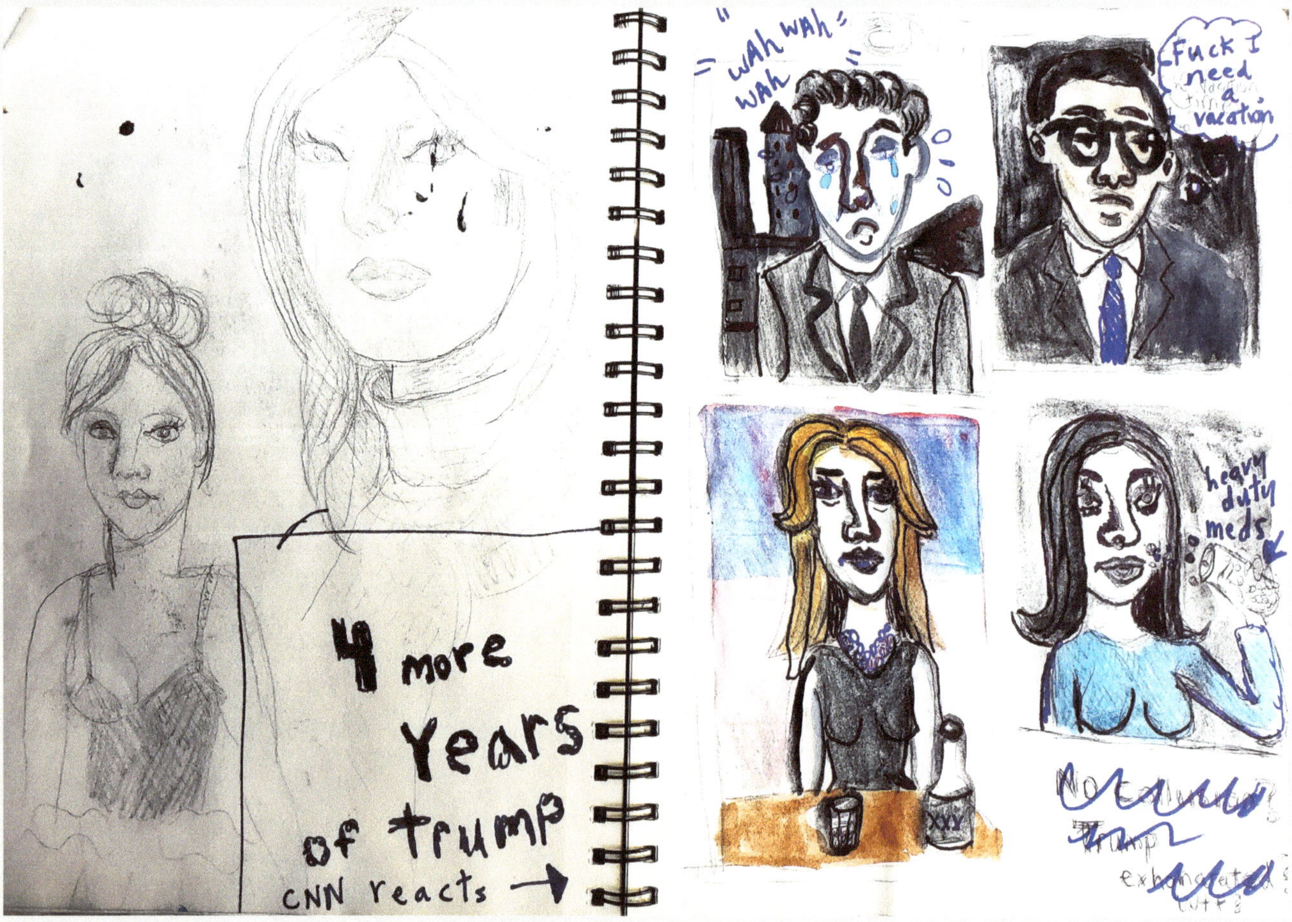
4 more Years of trump
CNN reacts →
"WAH WAH WAH"
Fuck I need a vacation
heavy duty meds

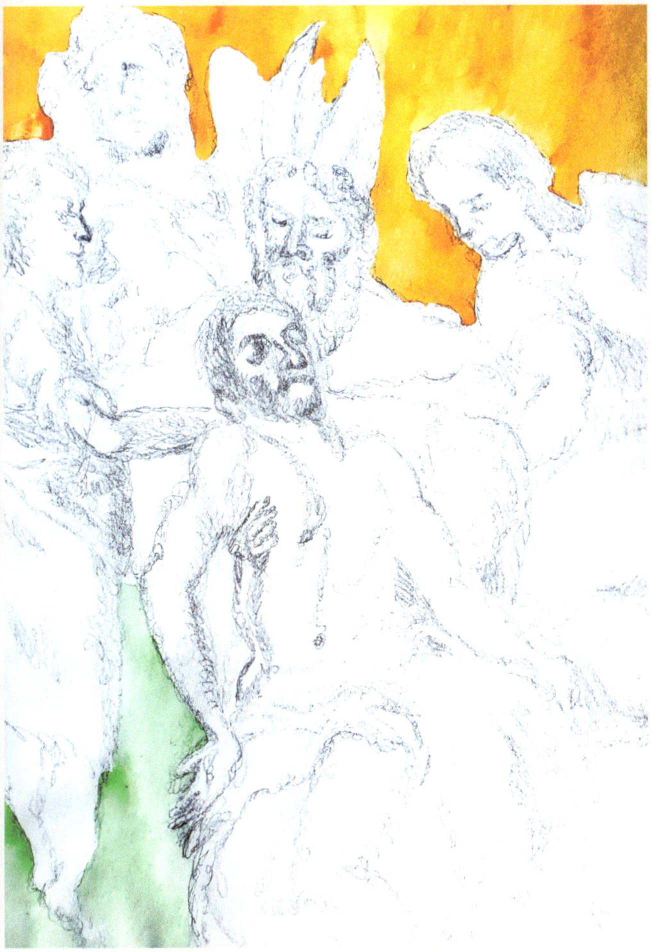

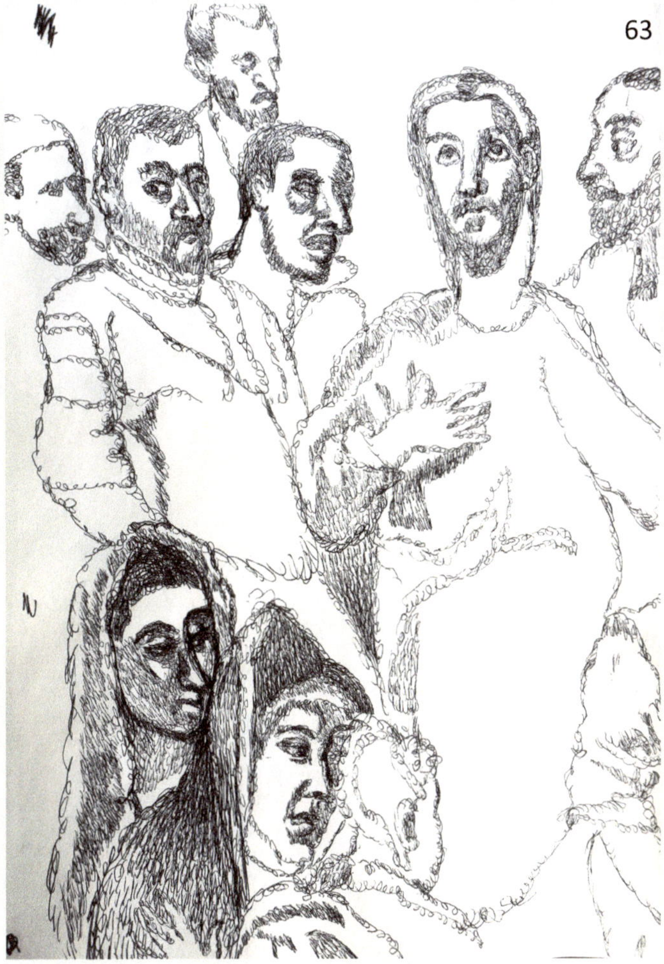

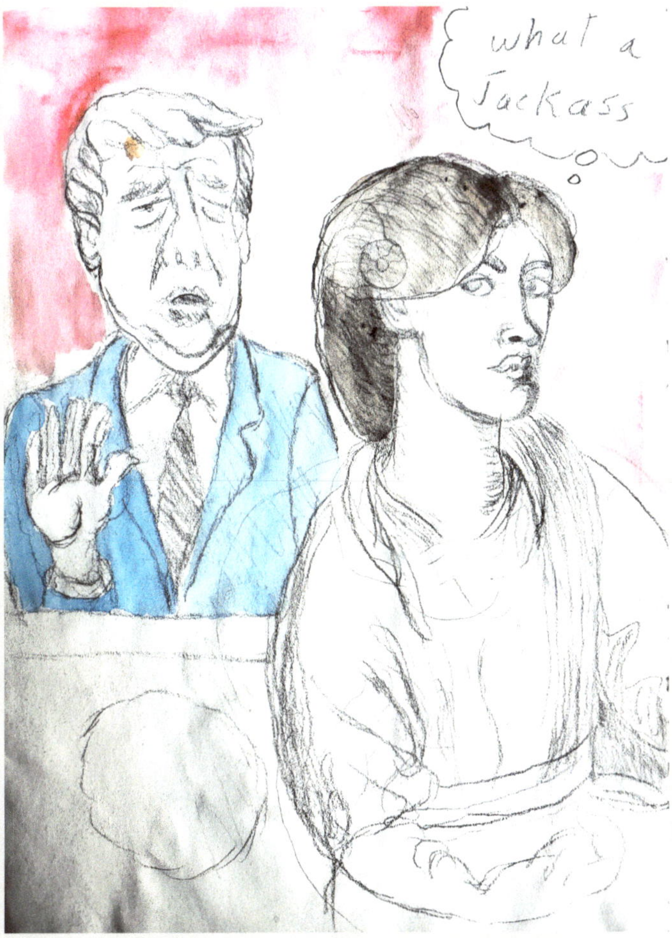
what a Jackass

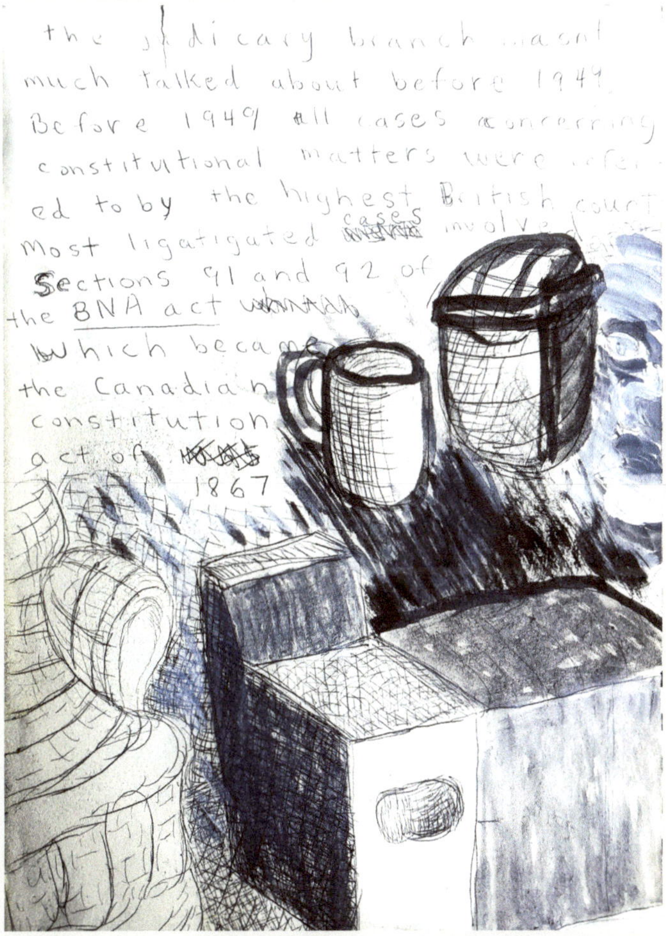
the judicary branch wasnt much talked about before 1949
Before 1949 all cases concerning constitutional matters were referred to by the highest British court
Most ligatigated cases involved
Sections 91 and 92 of the BNA act
which became the Canadian constitution act of 1867

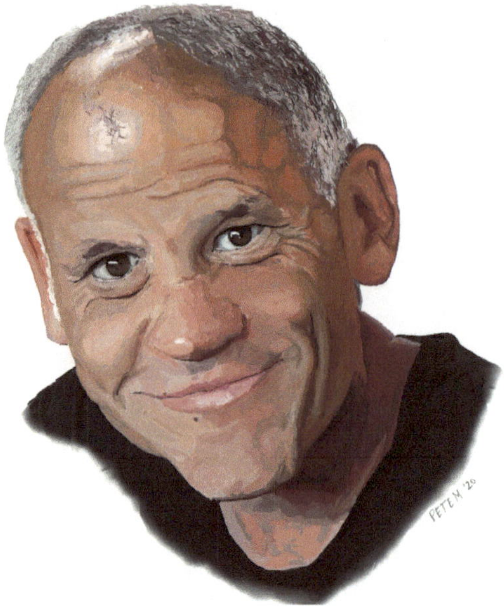

Peter Mitchell, *Bruce,* 2020. Digital painting

This book made available in print at cost and in PDF format for free. If you enjoyed Bruce's collection of artworks please consider making donation to the Mustard Seed Church Art Program in Edmonton. Without the Mustard Seed we would not have these creations.

https://theseed.ca/donate/

Please select Edmonton and mention the art program in the comments about why you are donating.

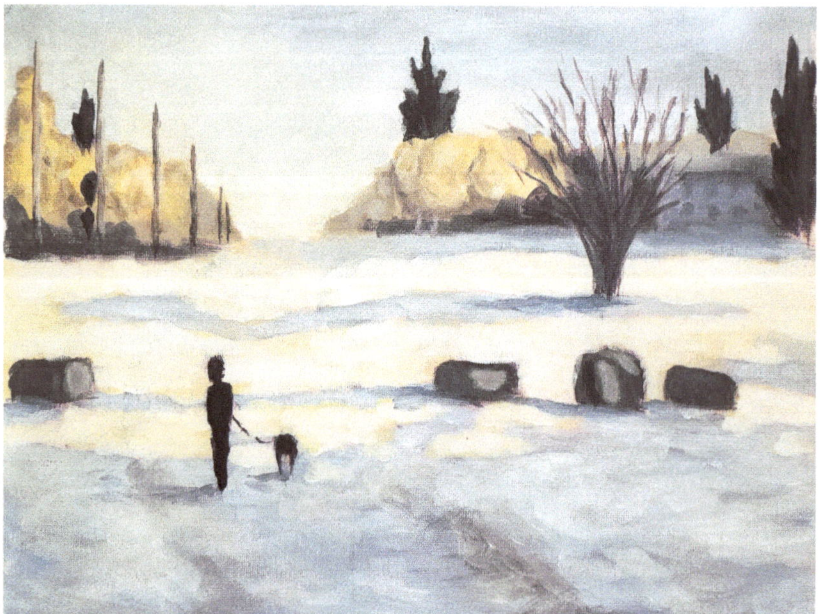

Mary Mitchell, *Bruce,* 2020. Acrylic on canvas

CPSIA information can be obtained
at www.ICGtesting.com
Printed in the USA
LVHW072004130121
676410LV00003B/11